Wednesday night in Sin City. Las Vegas, NV April 18, 2006.

FlipChip photo courtesy of LasVegasVegas.com

Approximately 606 players paid $25,000 to play against

TOPLESS GLITTER GULCH.
GIRLS OF LET US
GLITTER ENTERTAIN

the best in the Bellagio's Five Stars Poker Classic. Dealers

FlipChip photo courtesy of LasVegasVegas.com

anonymous players, stars, and big champions; they're all

ready for what the pros now consider the event of the year

In 6 days, 4 hours, Joe Bartholdi will win the $3,700,00. Not

to mention recognition from his peers. **Shuffle up and deal!**

ISBN: 978 2 7594 0166 6
Translated from the French by Molly Stevens.
English-language poker consultant: Brant Janeway.

Printed in Singapore

François Montmirel

POKER

THE ULTIMATE BOOK

ASSOULINE

Contents

SKILLS
STRATEGY
PSYCHOLOGY
LUCK

That's ❧Poker

When we think poker, we no longer think of cheats, cons, and shady characters. These clichéd cast of characters didn't stop poker from becoming the most played card game in the world. It has become a genuine social phenomenon.

How do you explain this success? Poker rules are very simple and its ingredients are explosive. It takes strategy, prediction skills, global vision, psychology, and luck, all of which can translate into staggering, impressive winnings that can even exceed ten million dollars.

For a long time, poker was classified among unfavorable games of chance (mostly because of a law). It is now recognized as a game of strategy and influence.

Whether you are a man or woman, young or old, professional or amateur, oriented toward psychological aspects or luck, you could beat the biggest poker champions. And even if you start with a little, you can rake it in big. To date, there is no other game like it.

Playing ❧

Poker and its ancestors radically strayed away from the first card games, which were mostly trick-taking games: players showed their cards and the one with the strongest hand won them all. A game would consist of a series of tricks, until players had no cards left.

In poker, this patient repetition was replaced by the concept of single hands. Instead of focusing on using his cards, the player focuses on accumulating winning combinations. Each game is a single combat, not several tricks.

In order to win, a player has to show a stronger hand than his opponent or opponents, based on ten types of hands of five cards each. But, a player can also win by forcing his opponent to pull out of the hand by making the game too expensive (see "Betting").

Hands are an integral part of games like dominos and dice, which came out of pharaonic Egypt, the Incan hypogeum, the Greek City, and the ancient dynasties of China. Centuries later, playing cards were flat surfaces for recording dice results.

THE VARIOUS HANDS OF POKER
IN ORDER OF DECREASING VALUE

10 ♠	J ♠	Q ♠	K ♠	A ♠	Royal flush
5 ♥	6 ♥	7 ♥	8 ♥	9 ♥	Straight flush
2 ♦	A ♣	A ♦	A ♥	A ♠	Four of a kind
K ♦	K ♠	A ♦	A ♥	A ♠	Full house
2 ♠	5 ♠	10 ♠	J ♠	K ♠	Flush
5 ♠	6 ♥	7 ♣	8 ♣	9 ♥	Straight
6 ♥	8 ♣	K ♣	K ♦	K ♠	Three of a kind
3 ♦	5 ♠	5 ♦	K ♦	K ♠	Two pairs
3 ♦	5 ♠	7 ♣	9 ♣	9 ♥	One pair
3 ♦	5 ♠	6 ♥	J ♦	A ♠	Nothing

"WHOEVER INVENTED POKER WAS SMART, BUT WHOEVER INVENTED CHIPS WAS A GENIUS."

At poker tables, chips replace real money with "fake money." At each table, a monetary value is attributed to a given quantity of chips (known as a buy-in). A thousand chips could equal a dollar at one table and a hundred thousand at another.

☙Betting

When single hands replaced tricks, the notion of compensation came into play: these are known as stakes. The sum is defined by changing bets that are increased when possible. Bidding implies bidding higher: a player can make his opponent pay more to continue in the hand. By doing so, he himself has to pay the same amount.

In poker's early days, the wealthiest players were also the most powerful ones: to win a hand without even needing to show his cards, a player simply had to bet a sum that the opponent could not afford. Cowboys in the Far West would bet using a kind of honor system. That is, a player only needed a trusty witness to guarantee his means.

To the great displeasure of No Limit purists—who hate to see stakes be capped—limits were established. These are known as table stakes.

Bluffing

As soon as showing your hand was no longer a rule, players could win a hand even if they were weaker than their opponent. This is an astonishing feat that is one of the keys of poker.

Bluffing

Bluffing is an even more sophisticated art than betting. If you don't have reliable information on your enemy, evaluate his strengths and weaknesses. The idea behind bluffing is to appear more threatening than you really are and make your enemy surrender.

The combination of betting and bluffing can prevent an opponent from calling you. In this case, the bidder is not obligated to show his cards, and he wins the stakes without having to prove he has the better hand. A smart bluffer can therefore win a hand even if he has the worst cards!

Counter-Bluffing

Accounts of head-to-head games long ago already refer to it: a counter bluffer pretends to be weak, so that his enemy takes advantage of him, and lowers his guard. It's at this point that he reverses the action, attacks full-on, and wins.

THE ART OF WAR

In the fifth century B.C., a Chinese general
named Sun Tzu wrote a book on military strategy,
which could be applied to other fields as well.
According to him, perfect strategy meant forcing your enemy
to surrender, not through fighting, but through observation,
deception, and mobility.
Drawing on his theories and calling a weak point "empty"
and a strong point "full,"
we can define four basic situations in poker:

**WHEN YOU'RE EMPTY,
COME OFF AS FULL
SO YOUR ATTACKER WON'T DARE TO ATTACK.**

**WHEN YOU'RE FULL,
COME OFF AS EMPTY
TO TRAP YOUR OPPONENT.**

**WHEN YOU'RE EMPTY,
COME OFF AS UNEQUIVOCALLY EMPTY
SO THAT YOUR OPPONENT SUSPECTS
YOU'RE IN FACT FULL.**

**WHEN YOU'RE FULL,
COME OFF AS UNEQUIVOCALLY FULL
SO THAT YOUR OPPONENT SUSPECTS
YOU'RE IN FACT EMPTY.**

Although it was written long before cards appeared in Europe,
The Art of War provides an excellent description
of different types of bluffs and illustrates the importance
of strategy and psychology in poker.

"ONLY BEGINNERS AND VERY GOOD PLAYERS ARE LUCKY."

It's a widely held belief that beginners have luck. But, with really good players, it's more about being able to take your chances at very specific moments.
When an opportunity arises, they've already seized it by calling. And when it doesn't happen, no one realizes it, because they've already folded.

❧Luck

People who think poker is nothing but luck are mistaken; if this were the case, a beginner would have the same chances of winning as an experienced player, like in roulette. In the long run, all players in poker have the same chances. What distinguishes winners from losers is sharp strategy and a focused psychological approach. The fact that certain poker champions play again and again in international tournaments is no coincidence.

Luck in poker isn't only about getting great cards. You have to know how to make the best of a good and unexpected hand. The things that determine the outcome of a hand (the position, the chip value, your cards, etc.) subtly come together to turn into a win.

Real champions know that big hands don't bring in big winnings. A strong hand (a four of a kind, a straight flush, a full house) will make your opponents want to fold early on. And in this situation, they won't be contributing to the pot. However, an average hand can be much more profitable for an experienced player, for he'll assume his opponent also has an average hand, although it most likely will be inferior.

Birth

THE ORIGINS OF CARDS

The most distant ancestor of playing cards seems to be ancient chips of wood used in China to write down dice toss results.

As early as the thirteenth century in the Middle East, players made their own cards from all kinds of materials. Drawing on traditional methods, they would cut out thick pieces of paper, fabric, leather, or papyrus and paint figures on them directly or with a stencil.

But it was Johannes Gutenberg and his development of movable printing around 1450 that account for cards becoming available and affordable for all.

"SPECIAL" CARDS

At first, the cardboard used for cards was poor in quality. Furthermore, cards were only printed on one side; they were not "tarotized," that is, they did not bear the same motif on the back. Anyone who wanted to cheat could make a faint mark on any card and "read" his opponent's hand like an open book.

Revolutionary cards, France, 1789–1799.

1450

THE ANCESTORS OF POKER

Glic was mentioned for the first time in writing in 1456 by the French poet François Villon. Similar to the German word *Glück*, which means "chance," a glic is a three of a kind, that is, three cards that match in value. Glic is played with two, three, or four players. Like in poker, it involves putting together the strongest hand while placing bets. But no cards are traded.

Flux comes from Italy, where it was popular as early as the fifteenth century. The principle of the game is similar to poker. A player places bets, but he can also skip his turn, the goal being to make a flux, a master hand consisting of three cards of the same suit.

Poch, from Germany, also emerged in the fifteenth century, and combined the notion of trumps, bets, and hands; for example, pairs, three of a kinds, and four of a kinds. Four players each receive eight cards from a deck of thirty-two cards and place their initial bets on a special board consisting of eight squares.

It is probably a game of *prime* that Georges de La Tour depicts in *The Cheat with the Ace of Clubs*, circa 1635. Immersed in his game, the player wearing the feathered hat does not notice the cheater exchanging a mediocre card for the ace of clubs hidden in his belt.

The Cheat with the Ace of Clubs by Georges de La Tour, Kimbell Art Museum, circa 1635.

AS SOON AS THEY EMERGED IN EUROPE, CARDS WERE PLAYED IN A VARIETY OF WAYS: AS A GAME OF TRICKS (*REVERSIS*), A GAME OF PURE CHANCE (*LANSQUENET*), A GAME OF CHEATING (*BONNETEAU*), AND A GAME OF HANDS (*GLIC*).

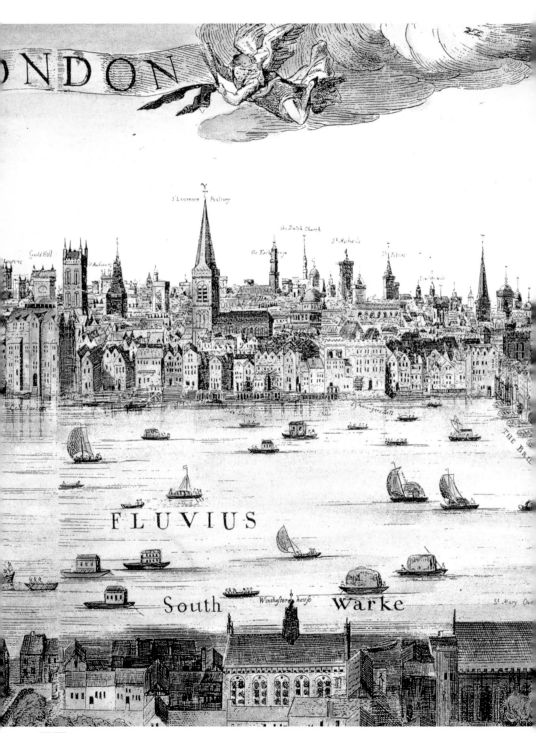

LONDON

St Laurence Poultney

the Dutch Church

Guild Hall   St Anthonys   the Exchange   St Michaels   St Peters

St Laurens

FLUVIUS

South   Winchester house   WARKE   St Mary Over

THE BRI

OF ALL THE ANCESTORS OF POKER, BRAG IS THE ONLY GAME STILL PLAYED TODAY. A GAME OF BRAG IS DEPICTED IN GUY RITCHIE'S FILM *LOCK, STOCK AND TWO SMOKING BARRELS* (1998).

The English game *brag* dates from the sixteenth century. Each player is usually dealt three cards from a deck of fifty-two cards. There are five hands: a *prial* (a three of a kind), a *flush run* (a same-color straight), a *run* (a two-color straight), a *flush* (a same-color hand), and a pair. Bets are made without exchanging cards.

Poque, which emerged during the eighteenth century in France, is related to the German *pock* and the English *pop joan*, which later became *bog* and *Pope Joan*. It is likely that French colonizers settling in Louisiana brought poque with them. Henceforth, it was practiced by Anglophones and pronounced as an English term. The game soon took on the name *poker*.

View of London Bridge on the Thames in 1616, details of an engraving from the time by Cornelius Visscher.

A GAME
TAKES A
TO LEAR
A LIFETI
TO MAST

THAT SECOND

N AND

ME

ER.

POKER
FACE

Having a "poker face" means having an unemo-tional expression, an impenetrable mask that hides either the strength or weakness of your hand. It is an attitude that the player's whole body takes on; it is the best way—indeed, the only way—to safeguard against involuntary feelings (see "The Tells") that might betray the hand. Often, other players use all kinds of strategies to try to crack the poker face; for example, they ask questions, repeatedly count their chips, or tell distracting stories and jokes.

Note: If you are tempted to use a poker face, concen-trate and don't let yourself lose your footing!

3 ♠

5 ♥

ON APRIL 9, 1682, IN THE NAME OF KING LOUIS XIV, THE EXPLORER ROBERT CAVELIER, SIEUR DE LA SALLE TOOK POSSESSION OF THE MISSISSIPPI VALLEY, WHICH HE NAMED "LOUISIANE" IN HONOR OF THE FRENCH MONARCH.

1682

IN THE NAME OF THE KING

In 1718, the regent, the Duc d'Orléans, inspired the name of the city that French colonizers founded at the mouth of the Mississippi. On May 14, 1804, an expedition of forty men, sponsored by President Jefferson, left the city of Saint Louis, located at the confluence of the Mississippi River and the Missouri River, in order to explore the unknown territories to the northwest. Their expedition would last two years and marked the beginning of one of the great founding myths of the United States: the Far West. It also started the colonizing crusade that would push the pioneers ever further west, all the way to the Pacific Ocean.

Robert Cavelier, Sieur de la Salle (1643–1687), the French explorer here in a Caddo Indian village, circa 1682. Painting by George Catlin, 1868.

NEW ORLEANS

ONCE IT PULLED AWAY FROM ITS AMBIGUOUS ORIGINS, POKER WAS TRULY POPULARIZED IN NEW ORLEANS. ITS FUTURE WAS TIED TO THE HISTORY OF THE CITY.

Having become the capital of Louisiana, New Orleans developed and prospered. Businesses were established and the city quickly expanded and filled with life. Its wealth drew the attention of pirates, mobsters, prostitutes, and gamblers, as was the case with all the great ports of the world. In 1748, the population of the city was estimated at six thousand people, two thirds of which were slaves.

IN 1812, THE FIRST STEAMBOAT SET OUT
ON THE MISSISSIPPI RIVER. IT WAS A FORTY-THREE YARD,
TWO HUNDRED TON SHIP NAMED *THE NEW ORLEANS*.
FROM THIS MOMENT ON, IT WAS POSSIBLE TO TRAVEL UP
THE TWENTY-THREE HUNDRED MILES OF RIVER AND REACH
REGIONS OF THE MISSOURI RIVER AND THE OHIO RIVER.

1812

SAINT LOUIS •

• MEMPHIS

DALLAS •

NEW-ORLEANS •

1820

THE STEAMBOAT ERA

THERE WERE SEVENTY SHIPS IN 1820. BY AROUND 1845, THERE WERE 560 STEAMBOATS, AND BY 1860, THERE WERE MORE THAN SEVEN HUNDRED.

At the end of the year, farmers would sell their bails of cotton in New Orleans. Their pockets filled with the fruit of their hard labor, the men, satisfied by good business, paid little attention to the timeliness of their return. Paddle-wheel steamboats were slow. It took several days to travel upriver. Therefore, a game of cards pleasantly proposed by a friendly and honest looking man was considered a godsend and accepted with pleasure as a way to kill time.

"7-11" PLAYING CARDS STEAMBOAT

Saint-Louis, Missouri
The waterfront crowded with steamboats

IF YOU HAVE
FIGURED OU
SUCKER AT
IS WITHIN T
HALF HOUR
THE SUCKER

N'T
T WHO THE
THE TABLE
HE FIRST
IT MEANS
IS YOU.

BEWARE OF APPEARANCES

THE HIGH AMOUNT OF TRAFFIC
ON THE MISSISSIPPI RIVER MEANT
THERE WERE MORE AND MORE
CHEATS ON BOARD THE STEAMBOATS.
JOURNEYS WERE LONG AND OTHER
ENTERTAINMENT NONEXISTENT, BOTH
GOOD REASONS TO PARTAKE IN
"A FRIENDLY GAME OF CARDS."

Soon, crafty cheats became staple characters on riverboats. Sometimes dressed as farmers and sometimes dressed in the latest fashions—in the manner of cleaned-up and charming dandies, for example—they shared one frightening talent: tricking unaware passengers.

Around 1830, there were about fifteen hundred "professionals" working regularly on the New Orleans-Louisville line that ran along some six hundred miles of river. It was said that you could count the number of honest players on your two hands.

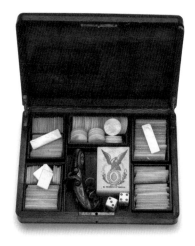

GAME BOX belonging to a riverboat player.

THE PROFESSIONAL POKER CHEAT'S
CODE OF HONOR

1 ★ The First Rule of Opportunism

Take advantage of what you've got: cards that are easy to mark, chips that are easy to hide, dark lighting, etc.

2 ★ The Second Rule of Opportunism

Take advantage of a player's weakness: naiveté, gullibility, poor eyesight, etc.

3 ★ The "Money Doesn't Smell" Rule

Take the money where it's at; don't worry about where it has been or who has it.

4 ★ The Rule of Polite Priority

If there's another cheat at the table, don't join.

5 ★ The Rule of Obstructed Priority

If there's another cheat at the table, ask him, during a break, if he wants to team up. If he refuses, don't insist.

6 ★ The Rule of Silence

Never admit you cheated, even when you're caught in the act.

7 ★ The Rule of Ultimate Survival

A small pistol in your jacket is a cheat's "fifth ace." Use only if truly necessary.

8 ★ The Devol Rule

If you're caught in the act, save your skin by telling a secret. Then skip town and never come back.

9 ★ The Hickok Rule

Never sit with your back to the door.

THE ART OF CHEATING

Manipulators

Dealing one card instead of another is the manipulator's basic trick. Knowing that an ace is on top of the deck (thanks to a mark on the back of the card), you just have to deal the second card and keep the first, giving it to yourself when it's your turn. Palming is another very simple operation. It allows you to get rid of one or several cards after giving yourself "too many" when the cards are exchanged. Changing decks is a fearsome trick. When the dealer takes back the deck after it has been cut to begin dealing, he substitutes this deck for another one he was holding in his other hand or in his sleeve. The switch is accomplished through a precise and rapid gesture at the table edge. The new deck is, of course, doctored to match your needs: marks, order, etc.

A distinctive sign shaped like a "7," going clockwise and located at the bottom left and top right of the card back, lets you identify the value.

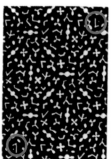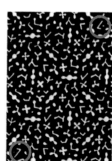

Device used to mark cards by slightly altering the corner.

Marking Cards

At first, the poor quality of the cardboard used to make cards made it easy to make subtle marks. A player who knew where the marks were could easily spot the important cards.

As early as the nineteenth century, unscrupulous manufacturers produced marked decks. Sometimes, a big cheat would flood a single city with hundreds of marked decks, so that, no matter where he went to play, he would be playing with his own cards.

A pair of pliers also could be used to make a little dent in a precise spot, marking the card in a tactile way instead of a visual way.

CANADA BILL
FRIEND OF THE PIGEONS

A PLAYER AND PROFESSIONAL CHEAT ON THE MISSISSIPPI RIVER IN THE MID-NINETEENTH CENTURY, WILLIAM "CANADA BILL" JONES CAUGHT ATTENTION WITH HIS SQUEALING VOICE AND HIS PERFECTLY INNOCENT LOOK. HE WAS THE IDEAL SUCKER. ALTHOUGH HE WAS RECOGNIZED AS ONE OF THE MOST TALENTED CHEATS OF ALL TIME, HE WAS A COMPULSIVE PLAYER. HE LATER LOST HIS ENORMOUS WINNINGS TO OTHER CHEATS WHO WRUNG HIM DRY.

Collusion

Cheats usually work alone. But they can also work in pairs. Pretending not to know each other, two players can play several times at the same table without being suspect. One of the two wins big, while the other loses a little. More characteristically, they communicate the value of cards using signals.

Tools

The most common tool used in the Far West was the "holdout," a kind of spring tied around a player's fore-arm that let him bring a card into his hand at the right moment.

Special guillotines were developed to mark cer-tain cards that, as a result, could be easily distinguished from the other cards by cheats in-the-know.

If you wore tinted sunglasses, you could see marks made with a special invisible ink that could not be seen by the naked eye.

HOLDOUT
One day, P. J. Kepplinger—a cheat who used one of the most sophisticated holdout models—was caught by his opponents. They agreed to spare him punishment by tar and feather under the condition that he give each of them their own device!

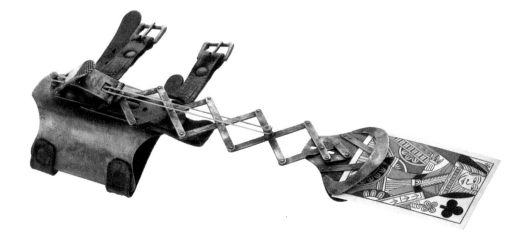

BLUFF

Bluffing is a strategy by which you convince your opponents you're doing (much) better than you really are: you compensate for a weak hand with aggressive betting.

A semi-bluff is slightly different: it involves betting high with a weak hand that nevertheless could improve (a straight draw or a flush draw, for example). If the opponent calls and if the next card completes your draw, you should have the better hand.

The definition of bluff can also be expanded to include making your opponent think you have a weaker hand than you do (see "Slow-Play").

DURING THE GOLD RUSH, GOLD WASHERS WERE OBLIGATED TO STAY ON THE PREMISES, WHICH MEANT THEY HAD TO SPEND A GOOD PART OF THEIR EARNINGS ON-SITE AS WELL, AT MERCHANTS WHO SOLD THEIR GOODS AT EXORBITANT PRICES, AND ESPECIALLY AT GAMING HOUSES AND BROTHELS.

Dice was the most popular game, especially since it took up little space, but faro, *bonneteau*, and, of course, poker were also widely played. It was not unusual that out of twenty houses built in a new pop-up town, at least fifteen were devoted to gaming.

Cheats were drawn to gold-digging areas because they thought that someone who spent his day searching for gold and filtering water would certainly become the ideal sucker come night.

Following spread:
Charlie Chaplin's *The Gold Rush*, 1925.

1848

ALL FOR GOLD

IN 1859, WHEN DENVER,
COLORADO, WAS JUST A
SMALL CITY COMPRISED
OF A BUNCH OF CABINS
OWNED AND BUILT BY
GOLD DIGGERS, THE
BIGGEST PLACE TO
GAMBLE WAS THE
DENVER HOUSE.

THE ELEPHANT CORRAL

Although the gambling house was originally too small for its activities, it eventually got so popular that it was renamed the Elephant Corral. There were always hundreds of spur-wearing cowboys there, ready to empty their beer mugs and play a game of faro.

Robert Teats, the owner of the establishment, would rent out tables and related accessories by the day, month, or year. That way, he wasn't held responsible for how honestly (or dishonestly) the games were played. Later, the Elephant Corral became a business center for miners and cards eventually disappeared.

The game simply involved betting on a pair of cards dealt by the «banker.» Because it was a fast, easy game, it was more popular in the saloons than poker.

Following spread : Players who preferred poker to faro put their name on a list. Sometimes they waited hours to play.

A JOB LIKE ANY OTHER

Aprofessional player could settle in a city that had several gaming houses and live from his winnings because he knew the game. Churches did not close their doors to him, which meant that the doors of heaven were probably open to him, too. However, as soon as he acted suspiciously or was suspected of cheating, he became the shame of the city. He was ruthlessly banned from houses and was sometimes even beaten, in certain cases, by the dupes he had cheated. Once identified, a cheat who was still alive only had one option: to get on his horse and get as far away from town as possible to save his skin.

THE PROFESSIONAL PLAYER WAS AS LEGITIMATE AND COMMON AS THE BLACKSMITH OR THE GROCER.

THE NUTS

Having "the nuts" means having the best possible hand at that time. The origin of the expression dates back to the time of the pioneers and the Far West. The "nuts" referred to the axle nuts from pioneers' carts. When a man would decide to gamble his cart—often his most valuable possession—he would literally remove the axle nuts and lay them on the table. This display meant he had the utmost confidence in his game because he was going all the way. Furthermore, the nuts assured other players that their opponent wouldn't be able to run away if a bluff failed.

When push comes to shove, if you have the nuts, it's fair play to show your hand or to say you've got the nut hand without waiting.

MAVERICK

RICHARD DONNER 1994

WILD WILD POKER

This fanciful film humorously depicted life in the old West as experienced by poker players. During this time, when any stranger could be either a sucker or a shark, nothing was off limits if it meant playing a good game.

Jodie Foster's character offered a glimpse into what women experienced as players in a world of cheating, tricking, and betrayal (see "Poker Alice").

WITH 124 EPISODES, *MAVERICK* WAS A HIT TELEVISION SERIES
IN THE 1950S AND 1960S. THIRTY-SIX YEARS LATER, THE
SERIES WAS TURNED INTO A MOVIE, STARRING JODIE FOSTER,
MEL GIBSON, AND JAMES GARNER (WHO PLAYED THE LEAD
ROLE IN THE SERIES), AND DIRECTED BY RICHARD DONNER.

THE CIVIL WAR

ALTHOUGH POKER ORIGINATED IN MISSISSIPPI, AND DEVELOPED BY TRAVELERS, BUSINESSMEN, MINERS, AND PIONEERS, THE GAME RIPENED DURING THE FIVE YEARS OF THE CIVIL WAR.

O nce the war was over, people in the North and in the South returned to their homes and brought poker, a favorite pastime on both sides, with them. The game was introduced into every level of society, to the point that it became one of the most influential elements of the reunified country.

Without the Civil War, poker would have probably remained a casino game played by outcasts. During the war, however, soldiers played the game during the long waits between battles, and this exposure catapulted poker into a new realm of appreciation and status.

The Battle of Nashville, by Howard Pyle.

6 ♦ 9 ♠

CARDS
WAR, I
DISGÚIS
A SPOR

ARE
NE OF
NET.

7
♦

2
♠

SHE MARRIED GAMBLERS AND SMOKED CIGARS. SHE CLAIMED TO HAVE NO INTEREST IN MONEY AND IMMEDIATELY SPENT WHATEVER SHE WON.

POKER ALICE

Born in England in 1851, Alive Ivers became an outstanding player by observing her husband, who was crazy about cards. Dressed like a princess, she took pleasure in facing off against coarse miners, who all did their best to avoid her. Faro, blackjack, poker: she played them all well. Onlookers attributed her feats to her unique ability to calculate her chances.

At age seventy-nine, her doctor recommended she have a bladder operation. "You'll deal," she answered. "I'll play the cards I get." And so she died, ruined, on the operating table on February 27, 1930, in Sturgis, South Dakota.

MADAME MOUSTACHE

In 1854, a twenty-something artist reigned over the scene at the Shasta House in Nevada City. Her name was Eleanore Dumont. It did not take long for her to figure out she could find gold without digging in mines; she opened her own gaming house and became "the angel of sin," stealing from poker tables. A dark downy line of hair above her upper lip gave her the nickname Madame Moustache. Far from hurting her, this odd feature greatly contributed to her glory.

7 ♦ 3 ♣

WILD BILL HICKOK WAS AN EXCEPTIONAL MAN, A LEGEND WITH A SOLID REPUTATION FOR HIS GAME, HIS DRINKING, HIS MOUNTED SALOON ENTRANCES, AND HIS FAST GUN.

DEAD MAN'S HAND

THE DEAD MAN'S HAND

This is the hand Hickok had when he was killed: A-A-8-8. The fifth card is unknown. Since that day, poker players worldwide have made sure that they face the door when they play. There's a superstition that if you have Hickok's hand, your end is near.

1876

Recruited by the North during the Civil War, he later fled to Kansas to lay low. By 1866, he was deputy sheriff in Fort Riley. He then became a scout in Custer's Seventh Calvary Regiment in 1868.

In 1871, his poker feats at Abilene, Texas, gave the Alamo Saloon its name. He became the town sheriff but was fired by the mayor for having simultaneously killed a citizen for a trivial matter and his own deputy by accident.

In 1876, he met Calamity Jane and headed out to Deadwood, in the Dakota Territory. There, he tried to practice an honest profession. But on August 2, while "Wild" Bill Hickok was playing a game of poker, a man named Jack McCall came toward the table and put a bullet in the back of his head. Hickok collapsed at the table and died on the spot. The murderer wanted to get revenge for his brother, killed a few years earlier by the "man of the law."

BETWEEN JUNE AND NOVEMBER 1896, POKER PLAYERS WERE LUCKY ENOUGH TO HAVE *POKER CHIPS,* THE FIRST MONTHLY ENTIRELY DEVOTED TO POKER.

POKER CHIPS

Available for five cents, every issue included sixty pages of stories, poetry, and ads, all, of course, focusing on the fascinating game. In the final issue, the publisher, Frank Tousey, announced that his periodical would henceforth be called the *White Elephant* and would cover stories about other games. The *White Elephant* was a collection of often colorful stories and interesting visuals.

Each cover featured a color lithograph and was radically different from the others.

October 1896.

POKER CHIPS

A MONTHLY MAGAZINE of original Stories.

FRANK TOUSEY

5 CENTS.

34 & 36 NORTH MOORE ST. New York.

CONTENTS

Adolescence

THE HOUSE
BEAT THE
IT JUST G
THE OPPOR
TO BEAT H

DOESN`T
PLAYER.
VES HIM
TUNITY
IMSELF.

STUD POK

EMERGING DURING THE CIVIL WAR, FIVE-CARD STUD IS THE FORM OF POKER STEVE MCQUEEN AND EDWARD G. ROBINSON PLAY IN NORMAN JEWISON'S FILM *THE CINCINNATI KID* (1965). IT WAS DIFFERENT FROM "CLOSED" POKER, POPULAR UNTIL THAT POINT, IN WHICH A PLAYER'S HAND REMAINED UNKNOWN BY HIS OPPONENTS UNTIL HE LAY IT DOWN.

FIVE-CARD STUD IS A GAME OF DISPLAY: IF THE CARDS YOU SHOW ARE THE STRONGEST ON THE TABLE, YOU CAN BLUFF WHEN RAISING THE STAKES, EVEN IF YOU DON'T HAVE ANYTHING ELSE. MOST OFTEN, ONCE A PLAYER SHOWS A PAIR, HIS OPPONENTS FOLD. STRAIGHTS AND FLUSHES ARE RARE SINCE THE PLAYER HAS TO CALL EVERY BETTING ROUND FOR A HAND HE HAS LITTLE HOPE OF MAKING.

ER

1 Each player is dealt two cards: one that is seen (a faceup card), the other not (a facedown card). The strongest faceup card starts the first betting round.

2 Each player calling in the first round receives a new faceup card. The player who has the highest faceup begins the betting round. Then, every player is dealt a third faceup card. And finally one last card. Every player ends ups with five cards: four facing up and one facing down.

3 The final betting round begins. If only one player remains in the game, he wins the pot without having to show his hand. If there are several players, they each lay down their cards. The best five-card hand wins.

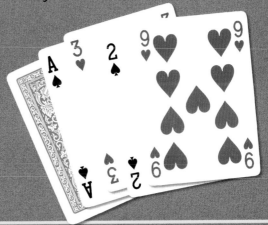

LAS VEGAS

A CONVENIENT STOP ON THE PIONEER TRAIL, A FREE ZONE, A MOB FRONT, OR A POKER MECCA, SIN CITY HAD TO BE SEEN.

1848

Founded by the Mormons in the mid-nineteenth century, the town of Las Vegas was a real oasis in the middle of the desert. At the time of the first California gold rush, it became a necessary stop for any traveler coming from the south or going back there.

The transcontinental junction between Southern California and Salt Lake City was completed in 1860. On May 15, 1905, Las Vegas, then only stretching over some one hundred fifty acres, received a train station. In 1911, the town's population totaled eight hundred regular inhabitants. San Francisco already had thirty-five thousand.

1860

IN 1910, PLAYING GAMES OF CHANCE BECAME
A CRIME IN NEVADA. BUT A PUBLIC PROSECUTOR
DECLARED THAT DRAW POKER WAS A GAME OF
STRATEGY; THEREFORE, THE ANTIGAME LAWS DID
NOT APPLY TO IT. THIS IS WHY, FOR OVER TWENTY
YEARS, YOU COULD PLAY POKER IN LAS VEGAS,
BUT NOT ROULETTE.

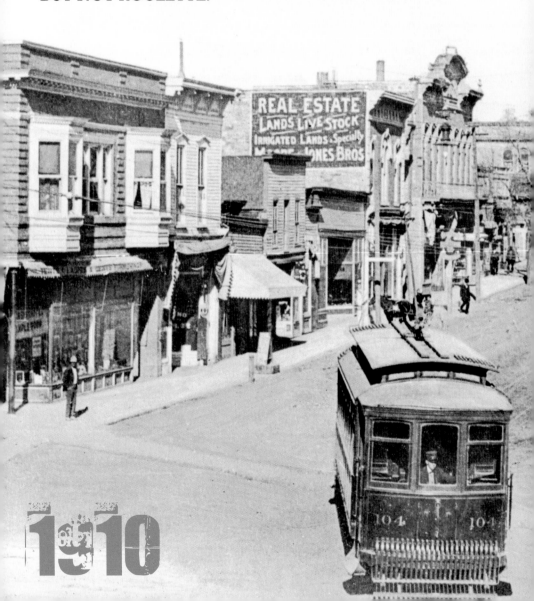

1910

1925

FREMONT STREET

LAS VEGAS

LAS VEGAS

THE WAVE OF LARGE LUXURY CASINOS STARTED AFTER WORLD WAR II. THE FIRST AMONG THEM, THE FABULOUS FLAMINGO, WAS FOUNDED BY THE MAFIA GENIUS BUGSY SIEGEL.

To build his project, he laid out a sum of five million dollars, a fortune at the time. Other casinos followed, springing up at a regular pace: the Last Frontier, the Thunderbird (1948), the Desert Inn (1950), the Sands, the Sahara (1952), the Riviera, the Dunes, and the Nevada Club (1955).

The 1960s were reigned over by Howard Hughes and the first giant hotel-casinos on the Strip—the avenue between the downtown area to the north and McCarran International Airport to the south.

BINION'S HORSESHOE

KEEPING A LOW PROFILE IN TOWN, POKER WAS MOSTLY PLAYED IN SPECIALIZED CLUBS. BUT THINGS CHANGED WHEN A FORMER MOBSTER FROM TEXAS NAMED BENNY BINION (SEE "BENNY BINION") TOOK OVER THE ELDORADO, QUICKLY RENAMING IT BINION'S HORSESHOE. STARTING IN 1951, THE CLUB BECAME THE PLACE FOR POKER AND HAD TABLES AT EVERY PRICE. FOR MORE THAN FORTY YEARS, THE EL DORADO SET THE STANDARD IN POKER, NOT ONLY IN LAS VEGAS BUT THROUGHOUT THE WORLD.

LAS VEGAS

IN 1970, THE WORLD SERIES OF POKER
WAS ESTABLISHED. IT TURNED LAS
VEGAS INTO A MECCA FOR POKER
PLAYERS EVERYWHERE.

1970

1980

Everything is huge in Las Vegas. Everything is colossal. New casinos like the Stratosphere, Treasure Island, the Mirage, and the MGM Grand represented major leaps forward in the world of poker and foreshadowed the Paris, the Bellagio, and the Venetian, among others. Las Vegas's population sprang from 185,000 residents in 1985 to 370,000 in 1995 to a million in 2005. And the city continues to expand, as if there are no limits.

ARRIVING IN THE MID-1860S,
AFTER THE CIVIL WAR, POKER
ONLY BECAME POPULAR
IN EUROPE DURING WORLD WAR I,
WHEN AMERICAN SOLDIERS
CAME WITH CARDS IN HAND.

POKER FINDS A HOME IN EUROPE

It was especially during the time between the two wars that poker became a household name.

It was immediately classified by different European jurisdictions as a game of chance, a dangerous game, "on par with roulette and ludo."

For those who could not organize private games at their home, there were clandestine gatherings. Billy Wilder's film *Irma la Douce* (1963), with Shirley MacLaine and Jack Lemmon, is a very realistic depiction of this era.

Poker was outlawed in Great Britain until 1960 and until the end of the twentieth century in other European countries.

Belgians playing cards in the street, Antwerp, circa 1938.

AS MUCH AS THEY LIKE NICKNAMES ("DEVIL-FISH," "THE GRINDER," ETC.), PLAYERS ALSO LIKE TO DUB POCKET PAIRS, THAT IS, HANDS CONSISTING OF TWO CARDS WITH THE SAME VALUE. THESE NAMES OFTEN COME FROM THE INITIALS OF THE CARD'S VALUE (E.G.: AMERICAN AIRLINES) OR FROM THEIR SHAPE (E.G.: CHERRIES).

A-A:	American airlines, pocket rockets, bullets
K-K:	King Kong, cowboys
Q-Q:	Double date, Hilton sisters
J-J:	Hooks, jokers
T-T:	Dimes
9-9:	German virgins, Popeye
8-8:	Snowmen, octopuses
7-7:	Hockey sticks
6-6:	Cherries, Route 66
5-5:	Speed Limit, nickels
4-4:	Magnum, midlife crisis, sailboats
3-3:	Crabs
2-2:	Ducks, deuces, Mini Me

1944

WORLD WAR II

Roosevelt had decided to propagate the New Deal beyond his homeland, and to turn American industry into "the arsenal of democracy." The American administration distributed more than thirty million decks of cards to its GIs, and "the boys" helped make poker known everywhere they went. In 1937, the rules of the game were even translated into Chinese. Several thousand copies were distributed.

The close-knit relationship between poker and history is now rather well known. But who knew that one of the most emblematic of soldiers to play was a certain Richard Nixon? He is said to have amassed a couple of thousand dollars during the war, which helped him launch his first congressional campaign in 1948 (see "Presidents At Play").

ALTHOUGH THE CIVIL WAR BROUGHT POKER TO ALL OF THE STATES, IT WAS WORLD WAR II THAT HELPED PROPEL IT AROUND THE WORLD.

THE CINCINNATI KID

NORMAN JEWISON 1965

The big card game, which takes up more than the last third of the film, starts with five players and ends with a ruthless face-off, pitting the young tiger against the man of experience. The battle turns in favor of the Kid, right up to the final moment when experience takes the upper hand. The tables turn one last time; it's spectacular and unpredictable, just like poker, going from one extreme to the next in a matter of seconds.

Directed by Norman Jewison in 1965, *The Cincinnati Kid* stars Steve McQueen (as "the Cincinnati Kid") who rivals Edward G. Robinson (as Lancey Howard). The film culminates in the final showdown between the two main characters.

THE COMMO
MISTAKE IN
UNDERESTIM
OPPONENT.
AT THE POK
ALL THE TI

NEST
HISTORY IS
ATING YOUR
HAPPENS
ER TABLE
ME.

When Winston Churchill visited Washington in 1946, Truman invited the British prime minister to a game. The more they played, the more Churchill lost. After a disastrous hour, the English head of state excused himself from the room for a moment. The other players, all of whom were American, gloated. But Truman asked them to be courteous, if not diplomatic, and let the cigar smoker win a few hands. The Americans were able to reduce Churchill's losses to a modest two hundred fifty dollars. This way, he couldn't return to his country claiming to have beat the Yankees at their own national sport.

PRESIDENTS AT PLAY

Harry Truman (President of the United States, 1945–1953)

Truman was a judge of the County Court of Jackson County, Missouri, when he began playing poker. One of his first opponents, Harry Vaughan, recounts that Truman loved to bluff. And when he would finally find himself alone in the hand after ousting his opponents, he would take naughty pleasure in laying down his hand, which clearly was not that strong.

Richard Milhous Nixon (President of the United States, 1969–1974)

Sent to the South Pacific during World War II, Lieutenant Nixon spent his time building landing strips and playing poker. "Nick" was always ready for a big game.

One day, he turned down an invitation to dinner from Charles Lindbergh, the famous aviator, because he was in the middle of a poker game. He later explained, "Our poker game was more than an idle pastime, and the etiquette surrounding it taken very seriously."

In his memoirs, Nixon seemed to minimize his winnings, which nevertheless helped finance his first congressional campaign, in 1948. He was thirty-five years old at the time.

"I LEARNED THAT THE PEOPLE WHO HAVE THE CARDS ARE USUALLY THE ONES WHO TALK THE LEAST AND SOFTEST; THOSE WHO ARE BLUFFING TEND TO TALK LOUDLY AND GIVE THEMSELVES AWAY."

Richard Nixon and the Whittier College football team, circa 1934–1942.

THE PROS RETURN

THE PROFESSIONAL POKER PLAYER IS A MAN IN HIGH DEMAND. PEOPLE APPRECIATE HIS SENSE OF HUMOR, HIS ABILITY TO REMAIN CALM AND BE SERIOUS ABOUT CARDS, AND HIS APPARENT ABILITY TO LOSE WITH A SMILE—WHEN HE LOSES. ACTUALLY, LOSING EVERY NOW AND THEN IS A NOT A BAD THING: IT KEEPS UP THE IDEA THAT HE ISN'T INFALLIBLE.

For a long time, Thomas Preston, Jr., aka "Amarillo Slim," was a *rounder*: a player who went from town to town, tracking down money making games.

The most common professional businessmen after World War II were called "high rollers." Coming from Texas for the most part, they were mostly interested in high stakes.

The Professional by Trade

He takes small risks, is bluffed more often than he bluffs, but is always able to win what he needs to make a regular profit. Unlike big-name professionals, all he wants is to win enough money to lead a decent life and have retirement savings for old age. He has a steady financial goal: every day he needs to win back the buy-in (the buy-in is the minimum amount needed to sit down at a table). As soon as he has won this sum, he stays in the game for another fifteen minutes, just to be polite. Then he nods to his opponents, gets up, and leaves the table.

The Professional Businessman

The professional businessman is another story. He has a comfortable nest egg and lives the big life. This club regular is often invited to play by patrons or ambitious players. A big player or a big-time gambler with a lot of money might take pride in beating a well-known professional. The professional seems to have everything—his reputation and his money—to lose.

A♦ Q♣ 5♦

POCKET PAIR ISN'T THE ONLY NICKNAME IN POKER. SOME HANDS ARE NAMED AFTER PLAYERS OR A PARTICULAR FEAT.

MOTOWN

A-K: Anna Kournikova

A-J: Blackjack, jackass

A-9: Chris Ferguson (the hand that won Ferguson the world championship in 2000)

A-8: Dead man's hand

K-J: Kojak

K-Q: Marriage (if the hand wins) or divorce (if the hand loses)

K-9: Dog

Q-T: Robert Varkonyi (Varkonyi laid down this hand three times in the finals to win the world championship in 2002)

J-5: Motown (as in The Jackson 5)

T-9: Countdown

T-2: Doyle Brunson (the hand that won Brunson two world championships in 1976 and in 1977)

7-2: Beer hand (the worst hand in Texas Hold 'em and so nicknamed for two reasons: (1.) because when you have it, it's always better to go have a beer, or (2.) because you would only play it if you've had too much to drink.

4-9: San Francisco (both a reference to the San Francisco pro football team and to the first Gold Rush of 1849)

3-8: Raquel Welch (so named because, for many years, Welch claimed to be thirty-eight years old)

BENNY

BORN IN 1904 IN PILOT GROVE, TEXAS, LESTER BEN BINION WAS THE TRUE FATHER OF COMPETITIVE POKER.

In 1926, he began playing at a craps club run by the mob in Dallas. Business was booming, but craps remained illegal.

Starting in 1938, the Mafia began to poach on his territory, but he remained influential. Although he was protected by politics, he had to pack up quickly in 1946 when his protection lost the elections.

He returned to Las Vegas, where he became the owner of the Las Vegas Club and, later, the Westerner Gambling House. In 1951, he bought the Eldorado and the Apache Hotel, merging them together to become Binion's Horseshoe.

Despite his shady career, Binion banned cheating in his club and encouraged a warm and friendly atmosphere. As the owner of the biggest casino in downtown Las Vegas, he founded the World Series of Poker in 1970, which soon became the most popular poker tournament in the world. He died in bed in 1989, adored by players worldwide.

In early 2004, Binion's Horseshoe went bankrupt and closed down. Harrah's immediately took over the establishment and bought the license for the WSOP.

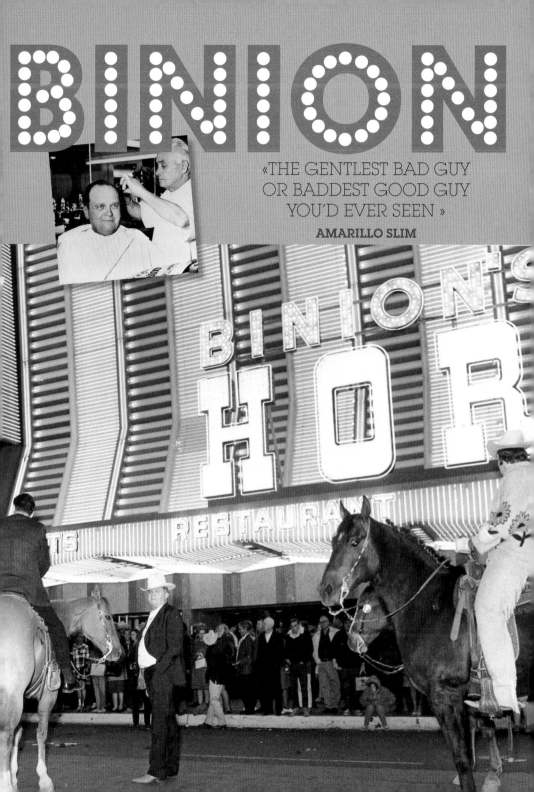

BINION

« THE GENTLEST BAD GUY
OR BADDEST GOOD GUY
YOU'D EVER SEEN »

AMARILLO SLIM

THE SWINDLE

The explosive ingredients of poker —money, adrenaline, taunts, lies, intimidation, sometimes even unlawfulness—are fertile ground for every kind of tampering, especially when you can identify a weakness in a potential victim. Today, tournament poker is so monitored that almost no game can be tampered with, though this was not always the case. There were all kinds of legendary swindles happening in back rooms where games were played.

A great example of the swindle is in David Mamet's *House of Games* (1987), in which a famous psychiatrist is the victim of a poker game gone bad—and she's not even playing.

> **"YOU HAVE TO LEARN WHAT KIND OF HAND THIS GUY SHOWS DOWN, WHAT THAT ONE'S MOVES, WATCH THE VEINS IN HIS NECK, WATCH HIS EYES, THE WAY HE SWEATS."**
> **JOHNNY MOSS (1975)**

THE TELLS

In the context of poker, "tells" are signs. If a player only plays with his chips before raising, that's a tell. A tell gives you a real advantage over an opponent. You can cut through some of the chance of cards by observing who you're playing against and noticing their tics and attitudes.

If a player curls up in his chair, if he leans over the table when he raises, or if he suddenly stops talking . . . these are all examples of behavior that are probably signs. It's up to you to figure them out.

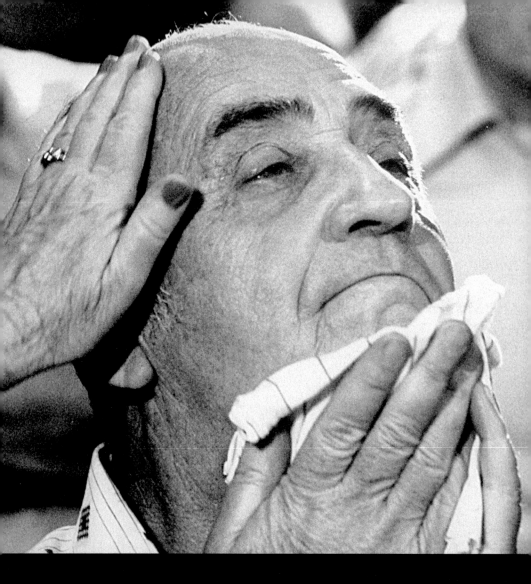

JOHNNY MOSS WON THE WORLD
SERIES OF POKER THREE TIMES, IN
1970, 1971, AND 1974. BY THE TIME OF
HIS RETIREMENT IN 1980, MOSS HAD
PLAYED AT EVERY WSOP FROM 1970
TO THE 1995 WORLD SERIES.

THE
GENTLEMAN
OF POKER

BORN IN 1907, IN TEXAS, JOHNNY MOSS BEGAN
PLAYING POKER AT AGE TEN. HE LEARNED
EVERYTHING THERE WAS TO KNOW FROM A GROUP
OF CHEATS: HOW TO DEAL FROM THE BOTTOM OF
THE DECK, HOW TO HIDE A CARD UP YOUR SLEEVE,

At fifteen, he found work that suited him: for ten to twenty dollars a day, he supervised tables, looking for possible cheats. For two years, he was immersed in a world of cards, never missing a moment of the show. This completed his poker education. He had found his vocation: professional poker player.

Moss always hated cheats, especially cheats who used a holdout. If he was suspicious, he would have his opponents strip naked. He found fifteen holdouts on men in their birthday suits.

He began working for Texaco so that he could play in the best games in East Texas, in the oil fields. The job was so lucrative, he quit after a few months with four thousand dollars in his pocket. He then moved to Graham, Texas, with more than a hundred thousand dollars. In the 1940s, he was known by all the big players as being one of the best.

But he didn't only excel at poker. He was also an excellent golf player with an eight handicap. On top of having a great game, he had psychological control. When a large sum was bet on a course, and when winning depended on the last hole, his opponent would sometimes lose his cool, but he never would. This is how Moss won millions of dollars in golf.

WHEN A MAN
MEETS A MAN
EXPERIENCE
WITH EXPERIE
WITH MONEY
WITH MONEY
EXPERIENCE.

WITH MONEY
WITH
THE MAN
NCE LEAVES
AND THE MAN
LEAVES WITH

« MR. MOSS, I HAVE TO LET YOU GO. »

ALMOST FIVE MONTHS AFTER STARTING THE TOURNAMENT, NICK DANDOLOS LOST A FINAL POT, GOT UP, SMILED AT HIS OPPONENT, AND SAID, "MR. MOSS, I HAVE TO LET YOU GO."

In 1949, Dandolos asked Benny Binion to find him a worthy opponent for a head-to-head tournament. Binion immediately thought of the biggest Texan high roller, Johnny Moss, his childhood friend.

Dandolos's tournament was special: it would end when one of the players requested it to. Binion quickly sensed the potential the event had for his casino. He decided that the tournament would take place behind glass, near the entrance, where it would attract the maximum amount of clients.

The game started with five-card stud, then continued with various kinds of poker: seven-card stud, closed poker, face-down poker, seven-card stud high-low, etc. Moss was younger than his opponent but he had experience with these variations. Week after week, he increased his lead and ended up winning the longest game in history. Reportedly, he raked in two million dollars.

A♦ A♠ 8♥

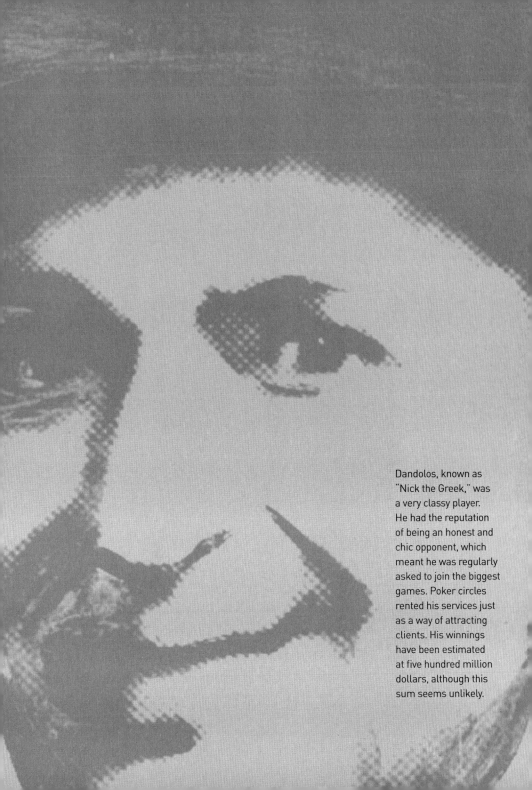

Dandolos, known as "Nick the Greek," was a very classy player. He had the reputation of being an honest and chic opponent, which meant he was regularly asked to join the biggest games. Poker circles rented his services just as a way of attracting clients. His winnings have been estimated at five hundred million dollars, although this sum seems unlikely.

BETWEEN 1970 AND 1990, THERE WERE FOUR IMPRESSIVE DOUBLE VICTORIES AT THE MAIN EVENT

(The "main event" is the most important tournament at the WSOP; today, this is the event most generally referred to as the world championship.)

⭐ In 1970 and 1971, John Moss won the first two years of the event.

⭐ In 1976, Doyle Brunson, an itinerant Texan, beat twenty-two players. The following year, he beat thirty-four; he missed making it a triple victory in 1980 after losing his final game against another genius, Stuart Ungar. Brunson holds the record for WSOP titles with Phil Hellmuth and Johnny Chan (ten).

⭐ In 1980, Stuart Ungar, known as "the Kid," won for the first time. He was twenty-seven years old. He won again the following year. He would again become world champion in 1997.

⭐ In 1987, Johnny Chan, known as "the Oriental Express," beat the competition, then repeated as champion the following year. He lost the triple victory by a hair in 1989. He was defeated in the final game by a younger player, Phil Hellmuth, who was twenty-four.

THE WORLD SERIES OF POKER (WSOP) CAME OUT OF THE LEGENDARY GAME BETWEEN JOHNNY MOSS AND NICK DANDOLOS. BEING THE BUSINESSMAN HE WAS, BENNY BINION WANTED TO TAKE ADVANTAGE OF THE ATTENTION THE TOURNAMENT DREW. HE HAD AN IDEA: WHY NOT ORGANIZE A HUGE POKER TOURNAMENT?

THE WSOP IS BORN

In 1970, Binion finally saw his dream come true. He turned to all the players he knew—mostly Texas high rollers—and asked them to participate in the first large-scale poker tournament. This tournament was varied: over a period of five days, a different kind of poker was played every day. The game ended when only one player was left, and when he had won everyone else's money.

During the first World Series of Poker, there was no money to be distributed. The winner was chosen by vote. Johnny Moss was elected the first world champion among thirty-eight participants.

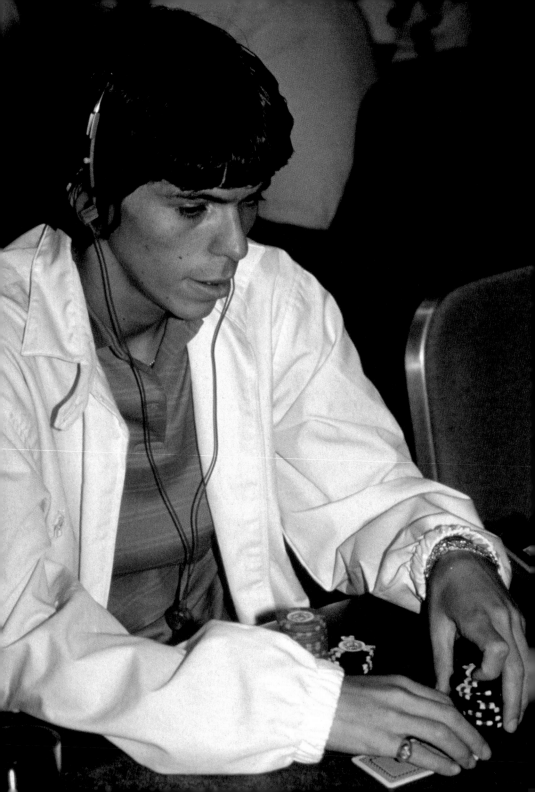

STU UNGAR
THE KID

AT A VERY YOUNG AGE, STUART ERROL UNGAR
LEARNED GIN RUMMY, WINNING HIS FIRST
TOURNAMENT AT AGE TEN. AT FIFTEEN, HE WON
TEN THOUSAND DOLLARS IN A GIN RUMMY
TOURNAMENT. HIS FAMILY AND FRIENDS WERE
CONVINCED: STU WAS A GENIUS AT THE GAME.

He discovered poker in Las Vegas and quickly cleaned out every table in town. Because he had an extraordinary photographic memory, he once bet a hundred thousand dollars against a blackjack player who didn't believe he could memorize a half a shoe of 312 cards. Ungar did it. He found himself banned from every blackjack table in Vegas. Either as an act of bravado or to impress, he bet enormous sums in fields he knew little about, as if to prove that not only was he a genius but also that he had luck on his side. He once lost fifty thousand dollars in golf when he was only a beginner; he had insisted he play against a top player.

After his two consecutive world champion titles, in 1980 and 1981, he became the man to beat in poker. After a long dry streak and a battle with drugs, he was back on track in 1997. He played in the WSOP and won for a third time, setting a record he still holds today. On November 22, 1998, he was found dead in his hotel room.

Stuart Ungar's physique served him well. He had a boy's face, was five foot four, and weighed one hundred ten pounds. Any opponent who didn't know him, tended to underestimate him.

DURING HIS CAREER, UNGAR PARTICIPATED IN THIRTY MAJOR TOURNAMENTS. HE WON TEN. THIS RECORD HAS NEVER BEEN MATCHED. EXPERTS ESTIMATE HIS TOTAL LIFE WINNINGS AT MORE THAN FIFTY MILLION DOLLARS.

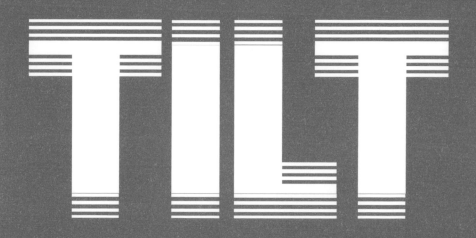

TILT

A player is "on tilt" when he lets his emotions affect the way he plays. This generally happens after a bad beat (see "Bad Beat") or because he's being taunted or is tired. He therefore becomes frustrated and annoyed enough that he "forces" his game, ignoring the most basic rules of caution and jeopardizing all or some of his chips.

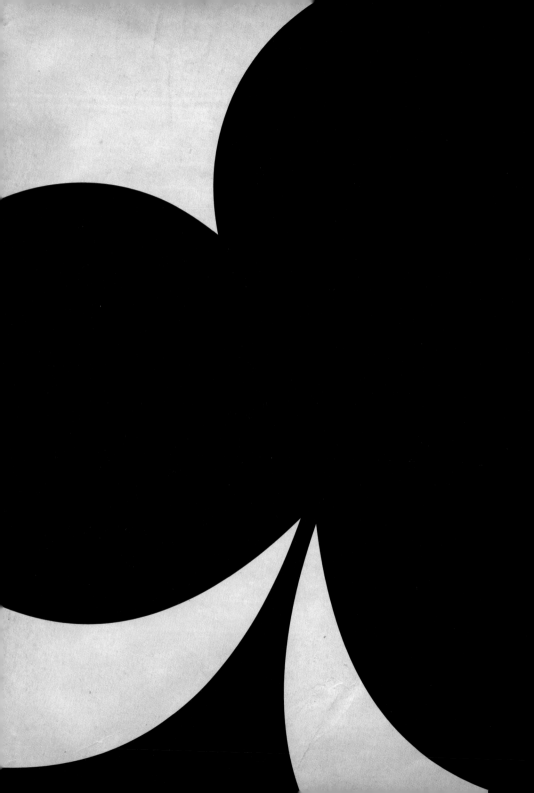

Maturity

PEOPLE THINK
THE SKILL IS
PART, BUT TH
THE TRICK TO
IS MASTERING
THAT'S PHILO

MASTERING
THE HARD
EY'RE WRONG.
POKER
THE LUCK.
SOPHY.

TEXAS HOLD

TEXAS HOLD 'EM (OR JUST HOLD 'EM) EMERGED AT THE TURN OF THE TWENTIETH CENTURY IN ROBSTOWN, TEXAS. JOHNNY MOSS WAS ITS FIRST GREAT PROMOTER. IN 1925, HE PROPOSED A NO-LIMIT VARIANT IN A DALLAS CLUB WHERE HE WORKED. TODAY, ALMOST 80 PERCENT OF POKER GAMES ARE A VARIATION OF TEXAS HOLD 'EM.

UTG

1

THE FIRST BETTING ROUND
The small blind or SB (left of the button) and the big blind or BB (left of small blind) bet. Then every player is dealt two "closed" cards (facedown).
It's the under-the-gun player (UTG)—the player seated to the left of the big blind—who begins. He chooses to:
- fold (get out of the hand)
- call (call the big blind and stay in the hand)
- raise the blind
At the end of this first round of betting, known as preflop, the hand continues, as long as at least two players remain.

'EM

SB

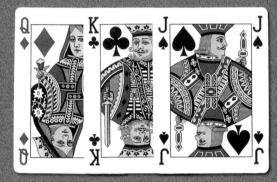

THE FLOP
The dealer burns a card: instead of dealing the card at the top of the deck, he puts it aside, and deals the three following cards, which he turns faceup ("open" cards). This is the flop. After a second betting round, which the small blind begins, the hand continues, as long as two players remain.

BB

TEXAS HOLD

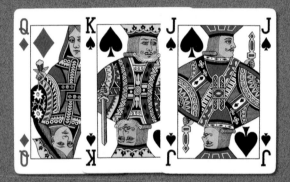

3

THE TURN
The dealer burns a card, then turns up the next one to the right of the flop. This is the turn, or fourth street. At the end of the third bidding round, the hand continues, as long as two players remain.

'EM

THE SHOWDOWN

The players still in the hand show their respective cards. This begins with the player to the left of the last player to raise. A player who feels he has lost does not have to show his hand, but he thereby loses any chance of winning the pot. A player can immediately show if he believes he's the winner, even if he was not the last player to raise. The pot goes to the best hand turned over. Players with equal hands share the winnings.

THE RIVER

The dealer burns a card, then places the following one to the right of the turn. This is the river, or fifth street. The flop, turn, and river together make up the board. At the end of this final round of betting, the hand continues, as long as two players remain.

PROFESSIONAL TOURNAMENTS

The WSOP (World Series of Poker)

Founded by Benny Binion in 1970, the World Series of Poker (WSOP) takes place in July and includes thirty to fifty tournaments; on average, one per day. The buy-in ranges from fifteen hundred to five thousand dollars. The WSOP ends with the WSOP Main Event, which lasts several days (the buy-in is ten thousand dollars). Since it was established, the number of participants has grown from twenty-five in 1970 to 8,773 in 2006 (see the appendix for WSOP winners).

IN COMPETITIVE TOURNAMENT POKER, THERE'S THE WORLD SERIES OF POKER (WSOP) AND TWO MAJOR INTERNATIONAL CIRCUITS, THE WORLD POKER TOUR (WPT), AND THE EUROPEAN POKER TOUR (EPT). THESE TOURNAMENTS ARE WIDELY TELEVISED, AND BRING TOGETHER HUNDREDS, EVEN THOUSANDS OF PLAYERS. WINNERS CAN TAKE HOME MILLIONS OF DOLLARS.

The WPT (World Poker Tour)

Founded in 2002 by Steve Lipscomb and Mike Sexton, the WPT is an annual circuit that includes more than fifteen tournaments. Rankings are established at the end of the circuit and the top players head to a final, giant tournament at the Bellagio Hotel and Casino in Las Vegas. The buy-in is twenty-five thousand dollars.

WORLD CHAMPION
The winner of each of these tournaments is given a world title and a WSOP "bracelet." The winner of the main event is given the WSOP world champion title.

The EPT (European Poker Tour)

In 2004, unhappy with the fact that the WPT tournament mostly takes place in the United States, European promoters decided to create their own circuit. The EPT is modeled after the WPT, with ten annual tournaments taking place within Europe.

The winner, Brad Daugherty, took home the incredible sum of one million dollars, making the WSOP the most lucrative competition among all sports.

FlipChip photo courtesy of LasVegasVegas.com

A♦ 3♠ 5♥

Slow Play

Bluffing with a huge hand is another strategy. In this case, it's better to call it a trap. It involves betting moderately as bait, but without raising suspicions. While it might incite your opponent to bluff himself, you could rake in his chips.

The slow-play strategy is risky, however, if it isn't perfectly mastered. Luring in opponents at a low price means they have a chance of improving their hand, and even beating you.

THE INTERNET INVENTS CYBER

GAMBLERS FROM YEARS AGO MUST HAVE DREAMED OF A FUTURE IN WHICH PLAYERS FROM AROUND THE WORLD COULD ALL BE "SEATED" AT THE SAME TABLE. THIS CRAZY DREAM HAS SINCE BECOME A REALITY.

The online poker adventure began in 1998, when Mike Caro, a poker professional and theorist, launched his virtual poker room at PlanetPoker.com and then ParadisePoker.com.

In a few years time, the market literally exploded. In 2001, two heavyweights came onto the scene, PokerStars and PartyPoker. They immediately understood how to exploit this unbelievable resource and soon made deals for live tournaments (real tournaments instead of Internet tournaments). The idea is simple. Both sides win: live tournaments authorize the site to organize qualification tournaments, and qualified players fill the ranks of live tournaments.

At the end of 2000, the founder of ParadisePoker tried to sell what he considered to be a faltering business for fifteen thousand dollars. But he found no buyers. He had to wait until 2004 to sell. He did—for 287 million dollars!

ON MAY 30, 2002, THE FIRST INTERNET POT TO EXCEED A MILLION DOLLARS WAS PAID TO A HAPPY WINNER.

FAKE CHANCE

There have been many complaints about the misappropriation of funds on sites and about shuffling errors. The fact that a cyber-player can receive up to three times as many hands as in a live game in the same amount of time does make you wonder about the odd coincidences that happen more often in online games.

"Cyber tables" offer new ways of playing poker. For example, "sit-and-go" tournaments: instead of starting on a precise day, at a precise time, this kind of tournament begins as soon as there are enough players.

But the power of online playing lies in its capacity to have qualified tournament players compete in big live tournaments, like the WSOP. The fact that there are so many players makes this possible: hundreds of players each pay a modest sum (a few dollars) to participate in the online tournament. The top players win their "ticket" to the live tournament.

ROUNDERS

JOHN DAHL 1998

SMALL-TIME POKER

This movie sheds light on present-day poker professionals and their hardships: the daily drudgery, cheating, the Mafia and, finally, competition, which is Mike's ultimate goal.

Mike, a feisty little poker player, is played by Matt Damon. John Malkovich plays his opponent, Teddy KGB. John Turturro is a professional, and Edward Norton, a cheat.

"HERE, ALL THE GUYS WILL TELL YOU. YOU PLAY TO MAKE A LIVING. IT'S A JOB LIKE ANY OTHER. IT'S NOT ABOUT LUCK. WHEN IT'S GOING GOOD, YOU GET YOUR MONEY, IF NOT, YOU PROTECT YOURSELF AND KEEP IT LOCKED UP."

DOYLE
BRUNSON

A SYMBOL OF COMPETITIVE POKER'S EARLY YEARS, THE AUTHOR OF *SUPER SYSTEM*—THE MOST SUCCESSFUL BOOK ON POKER—AND A MULTI-TROPHY WINNER WHO HAS STOLEN TITLES FROM OPPONENTS YOUNG ENOUGH TO BE HIS GRANDKIDS, DOYLE BRUNSON IS A LIVING MONUMENT OF POKER.

He chose the fast track at an early age. It was a bumpy road, living the life of a rounder, making his way through Texas in search of the "juiciest" games. He was quickly nicknamed "Texas Dolly," and learned the ropes on the seedy side of Fort Worth, where he worked his way through illegal and dangerous clubs.

TODAY, WHEN DOYLE BRUNSON, AGE SEVENTY-FOUR, LEAVES THE ROOM AFTER LOSING, HE GETS A STANDING OVATION.

When he started traveling, he met two other professionals, Sailor Roberts and Amarillo Slim. They formed a partnership to hold off many of the profession's difficulties: being arrested (since professional playing is illegal), being cheated, being robbed or racketeered, etc.

Brunson has had great success in competition, including two world championship titles at the WSOP, in 1976 and 1977, and ten WSOP bracelets (a record). He won the last one in 2005.

"TRY TO DECIDE HOW GOOD
YOUR HAND IS AT A GIVEN MOMENT.
NOTHING ELSE MATTERS. NOTHING!"

DOYLE BRUNSON

A bad beat is the poker player's worst pet peeve. It's when you lose even though your hand "should" have won. But it didn't happen. A bad card comes out of nowhere; against all the odds, a hand comes from outer space.

A player has got to know how to "win" a bad beat and avoid getting "on tilt," if he wants to come back. And never forget:

"BAD BEATS ONLY HAPPEN TO GOOD PLAYERS."

JOE CROW

A ♦ 4 ♠ 5 ♥

POKER IS LIK[E]
EVERYONE IN
THINKS THEY
BEST AT IT...
A FEW ACTU[ALLY]
WHAT THEY

E SEX ...
THE WORLD
ARE THE
BUT ONLY
ALLY KNOW
ARE DOING.

SATELLITE GAMES EMERGED AT THE WSOP IN 1983. THAT
YEAR, THE MAIN EVENT FEATURED A HEADSUP MATCH-
UP BETWEEN ROD PEATE AND TOM MCEVOY. MCEVOY
WAS THE FIRST MAIN EVENT WINNER TO EARN HIS BUY-IN
THROUGH A SATELLITE TOURNAMENT.

THE SATELLITE CRAZE

SATELLITE GAMES ARE TOURNAMENTS IN WHICH THE WINNINGS AREN'T CASH, BUT RATHER "ENTRY TICKETS" INTO MAJOR TOURNAMENTS. THERE ARE AN UNLIMITED NUMBER OF PARTICIPANTS; THE MORE PLAYERS THERE ARE, THE MORE PLACES THERE ARE TO WIN.

On the Internet, satellite games are an even bigger phenomenon, because of the huge number of players involved. Internet games generally have a relatively low buy-in and satellite games are no exception, except that instead of there being two hundred players, there are two thousand!

There's nothing to be ashamed about playing in a satellite game. On the contrary! Even professionals play in satellites, live or on the Internet, when their sponsors won't pay their buy-in for a major tournament.

There are so many possibilities on the Internet that the satellite system can be full of surprises. A huge tournament can have a satellite with a two hundred dollar buy-in, known as rank 1. The site might organize a rank 2 satellite game, with a ten dollar buy-in, with access to rank 1. And if the site wants to cast a wide net, there might also be a rank 3, with a dollar buy-in and access to rank 2.

AMERICAN DREAM

THAT A SMALL-TIME ACCOUNTANT FROM NASHVILLE COULD CLEAR THE WAY FOR A NEW ERA IN POKER, AND THAT ON TOP OF IT, HIS NAME IS MONEYMAKER, SEEMS LIKE THE STUFF OF FAIRY TALES. IN FACT, IT'S A TWENTY-FIRST-CENTURY VERSION OF THE UNSHAKABLE AMERICAN DREAM.

Before the start of the tournament, Moneymaker was so short on cash, he almost sold his WSOP seat for ten thousand dollars.

In 2003, Chris Moneymaker won the WSOP world championship. He had never set foot in a tournament before. He only played on the Internet. By qualifying for thirty-nine dollars on PokerStars.com. he won his place in a qualification tournament for the world championship, which he then won, taking home two and a half million dollars.

Without knowing it, Moneymaker was great advertising for online cardrooms: "Play online? You could become a world champion!" PokerStars took this accountant-turned-champion and made him their poster boy. It mostly benefited the site.

"IF IT WERE EASY, EVERYONE WOULD DO IT."
BONNIE DAMIANO

$ 2 500 000

CELEBRITIES JOIN IN

David Schwimmer, Martin Sheen, Mimi Rogers, James Woods, Paris Hilton, Matthew Perry, Angie Dickinson, Dennis Rodman, Meat Loaf, and Michael Vartan are all recognizable regulars in big tournaments. Jennifer Tilly, Ben Affleck, Tobey Maguire, and Patrick Bruel from France even hold titles or WSOP brace-lets. Celebrities got their own tourna-ment in 2003: *Celebrity Poker Showdown*. And every player gets paid, as if it were a television series.

EVER SINCE POKER HAS BECOME GLAMOROUS,
A SYNONYM FOR DRAMA IN THE PUBLIC EYE,
AGENTS NO LONGER TRY TO STOP THEIR STARS FROM
MAKING APPEARANCES. ON THE CONTRARY.
EVEN JAMES BOND HAS JOINED IN.

Although the remake of *Casino Royale* doesn't revolve around poker, it does play a central part. It sometimes even steals the show. A luxury casino, quality players, huge pots and even bigger stakes. It's all about the "theater of poker."

"IT'S UNLUCKY TO BE SUPERSTITIOUS."

DAVE ENTELES

NEW ACCESSORIES

UNUSUAL ACCESSORIES HAVE BEEN POPPING UP AROUND COMPETITION TABLES RECENTLY. IT'S GOTTEN TO THE POINT THAT TOURNAMENT ORGANIZERS ARE WONDERING IF THEY'RE GOING TO HAVE TO LAY DOWN SOME RULES TO PREVENT THE PHENOMENA FROM GETTING OUT OF HAND.

HOODS

One time, as a joke, Phil Laak pulled on his hood to hide from an opponent who was scrutinizing him. He has taken it off since. Many players have adopted the look.

SHADES

The eyes are windows onto your mind; they indicate what's stirring. Players have never debated whether sunglasses should be banned or not. In any case, champions without outnumber champions with.

WALKMANS

With a Walkman, players hole themselves away even more. Often, when a hand gets technical, players will put down their headphones and study their cards, chips, and opponents ... as if they couldn't do so while listening to music.

CAPS

But what are all the cap-wearing players doing around the table? The answer is simple: they're protecting themselves from the hot lamps they sit under for hours and hours. Or maybe they're advertising their sponsor!

CHARMS

Really good players almost never have them. The rest almost always do: a lucky chip, a picture of their kid, an old figurine. These charms can also cover cards in case of a dealing error.

POCKET FANS

At first, they were used to blow away smoke. You don't seem them as often now, since most tournaments have become no-smoking events.

ADVERTISEMENT

More and more, players are being sponsored by online poker Web sites. To play, they agree to wear the logo. But limits have been set: no logo can exceed two and a half inches.

A 5 4

FlipChip photo courtesy of LasVegasVegas.com

A 5 5
♠ ♣ ♦

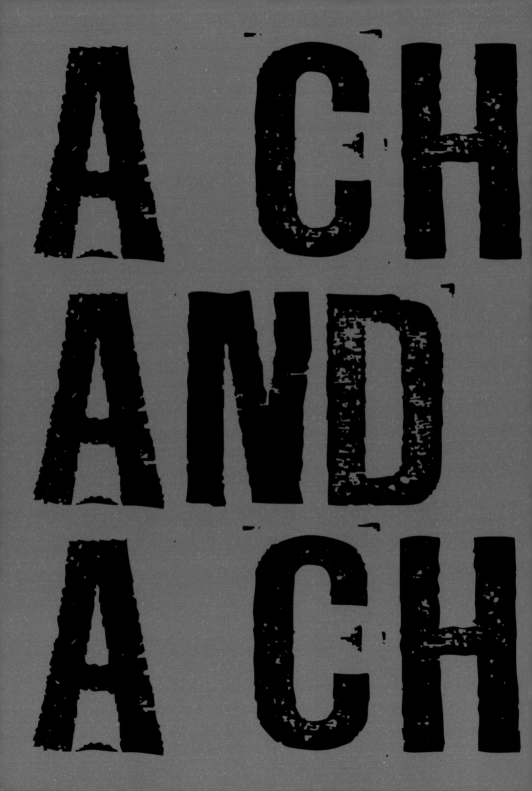

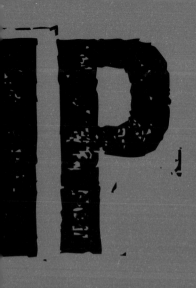

ALL YOU NEED IS A CHIP AND A CHAIR TO WIN. DURING THE 1982 MAIN EVENT, AT A POINT THAT HE THOUGHT HE WOULD BE ELIMINATED, JACK STRAUS FOUND A LAST FIVE HUNDRED DOLLAR CHIP UNDER A PAPER NAPKIN. HE ENDED UP WINNING THE WORLD CHAMPIONSHIP!

7 CARD STUD

THERE'S ALSO A SEVEN-CARD VERSION OF STUD POKER. IN THIS VARIANT, THERE ARE NO "COMMUNITY" CARDS AT THE CENTER OF THE TABLE FOR PLAYERS TO USE.

SEVEN-CARD STUD CAN ALSO BE PLAYED HIGH-LOW: THE POT IS SPLIT IN TWO BETWEEN THE STRONGEST AND WEAKEST HANDS (THIS CAN SOMETIMES BE THE SAME PLAYER!).

1

Three cards are dealt to each player, two closed cards (facedown) and one open card (faceup). The lowest-ranking upcard proceeds with betting. In the following betting round, the highest-ranking upcard will start.

2 Each player is dealt three additional cards with a new betting round. Each player can bet, call, raise, or fold.

3 A fourth and final card is dealt facedown to every player still in the hand. In the end, players have seven cards: two down, four up, one down. The best five-card hand wins.

DEALER

OMAHA

OMAHA POKER COMES RIGHT OUT OF TEXAS HOLD 'EM. THE DIFFERENCE IS THAT EACH PLAYER GETS FOUR FACEDOWN CARDS INSTEAD OF TWO. FOR HIS FINAL HAND, THE PLAYER HAS TO USE TWO OF HIS DOWN CARDS AND THREE FROM THE BOARD.

THE FIRST BETTING ROUND
When every player has been dealt four cards, all down, the first betting round begins. The following rounds are the same as in Texas Hold 'em.

FLOP
The dealer flops the three community cards, faceup. Then, the second round of betting begins.

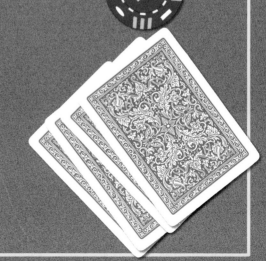

3

TURN
A fourth up card (turn) is dealt next to the flop. It is followed by a third round of betting.

4

RIVER
The fifth and last card (river) is dealt next to the first four. This is the board.

5

SHOWDOWN
After a final round of betting, players show their respective hands to compare. The best five-card hand wins.

HEADS-UP

THE MOST FAMOUS HEADS-UP DUAL DATES BACK TO 1949: DANDOLOS AGAINST MOSS. AFTER FIVE MONTHS OF NONSTOP COMBAT, MOSS WON THE HAND AND TWO MILLION DOLLARS. PLAYING HEAD-TO-HEAD HAS BECOME A WIDESPREAD TREND IN INTERNET POKER.

The newest fad is having each player only confront a single opponent, which limits choices and simplifies strategy. This kind of play is called heads-up. Incessantly attacking can pay-off, since it destabilizes an inexperienced player and makes him go on tilt. So can half-truths. Some players excel in avoidance strategies, which wear down attacks. Others, on the other hand, counter-attack, which can successfully throw off an aggressive opponent.

Since 2001, Andy Beal, the American billionaire and math and banking genius, has challenged the world's best players to play heads-up for forty million dollars. These pros gather at the Corporation every year and elect their representative. Rumor has it that through these games, Beal wanted to develop software for statistically perfect poker.

"PERCEPTION IS REALITY."
EMMANUEL KANT

Stack management is Boolean. Logically, chips you don't have are chips your opponent does have, and vice versa:

- If each player starts with a thousand chips, you know that five hundred equals a quarter. If you double your chips, you equalize.

- If you have a third of the chips, and you double, you'll take back the lead.

- If you have less than a quarter of the chips, even if you double up, you'll improve your position, but you won't take the lead.

A♦ 6♣ 3♥

Going all-in means betting all your chips. The action is an intimidating tactic, because it pulls the rug out from under your opponent, who can't raise afterward. He could fold, which is the ideal choice, but disappointing for an aggressive player. Or he could call, a decisive choice, if he thinks he can eliminate his opponent.

Going all-in is the only effective attack to make with a small stack. If you're called and you win the hand, you double your stack, which can be a lifesaver. If you lose, you're through, but at least you gave it your all.

T.J. CLOUTIER

THOMAS J. CLOUTIER, BORN IN 1939 IN ALBANY, CALIFORNIA, BEGAN PLAYING POKER AT AGE SEVENTEEN WHILE WORKING AS A GOLF CADDY. HE IS KNOWN TODAY AS ONE OF THE BEST PLAYERS ON THE PROFESSIONAL CIRCUIT.

When he turned forty, Cloutier moved to Texas to work on oil rigs. It was then that he started playing poker again and realized he could earn more money playing full-time than he could on the derricks.

At the 1985 WSOP, he came close to winning the title, finishing second to Bill Smith. He waited two years before taking his first big victory at the 1987 WSOP in the one thousand dollar Pot Limit Omaha event. Cloutier was named Poker Player of the Year in 1998 and 2002.

"THE ALBANY COWBOY"
T. J. "the Albany Cowboy" Cloutier has a phenomenal memory. Twenty years after facing an opponent in a tournament, even if he's forgotten the opponent's name, he'll remember the player's style. If he takes a quick look at a half deck of cards and someone asks what the seventeenth card is, he can call it without fail.

"THE BIGGEST MISTAKE TOURNAMENT PLAYERS MAKE IS GETTING THEMSELVES ELIMINATED BY THROWING THEMSELVES INTO POINTLESS RAISES."

A 6 6

PHIL HELLMUTH

PHIL HELLMUTH BECAME WORLD CHAMPION AT THE WSOP IN 1989. HE WAS THE YOUNGEST PLAYER, AT TWENTY-FOUR, TO DO SO. HE HOLDS THE RECORD TO THIS DAY. HE HAS WON MORE THAN FIFTY MAJOR TOURNAMENTS.

What's most amazing is his regular appearance in tournaments: he hasn't missed a single year since he took home the top honor. He has won ten WSOP bracelets in twenty-five years, a record he shares with Doyle Brunson and Johnny Chan. Although he's made it several times to the final table of the WPT, he's never won the title.

Hellmuth doesn't hide his ambitions. He wants to become the greatest player in the world. One day he may, even if it's unlikely he'll dethrone legends like Brunson and Ungar. He publishes a book every eighteen months, and there is a soon-to-be-released biopic about his experiences in the poker world called *The Madison Kid*.

"THE POKER BRAT"

Phil "Poker Brat" Hellmuth's image has evolved over the years. In the beginning, he was discreet and friendly, but he's become increasingly impulsive and whining. He's so sensitive that he even calls himself a poker brat. And yet he's a talented and instinctive player, known for his sometimes flagrant mistakes, but also dreaded for his unrivaled strokes of genius.

"POKER IS 100 PERCENT SKILL AND 50 PERCENT LUCK."

A♦ 6♣ 9♦

PHIL IVEY

IT'S TRUE PHIL IVEY HAS NEVER WON THE WSOP WORLD CHAMPIONSHIP. BUT HE HAS WON THREE WSOP BRACELETS IN ONE YEAR.

His grandfather taught him poker when he was a kid. He wanted to show him the dangers of the game but instead only peaked the youngster's curiosity. As a teenager, he told anyone who'd listen that he was going to become a professional player. His family disapproved and wanted him to have a different future. At eighteen, a fake ID got him into Atlantic City. At twenty, he moved there.

In 2000, he won his first WSOP bracelet, shortly after his twenty-first birthday. It was in the twenty-five hundred dollar Pot Limit Omaha event, and he beat Amarillo Slim, Devilfish, and Phil Hellmuth at the final table. He then moved to Las Vegas to become, in 2002, one of the most feared cash-game players in town. It was that same year that he won three WSOP bracelets. He won another in 2005.

"THE TIGER WOODS OF POKER"
Considered the Tiger Woods of the poker world, Phil Ivey is a discreet, friendly player and terrifyingly efficient. He also has an uncommon attitude: he never wears sunglasses and his expression never changes, whether he's totally bluffing or has the nuts.

"MY GOAL IS TO WIN THIRTY WSOP BRACELETS IN MY LIFE!"

JOHNNY CHAN

JOHNNY CHAN HAS BEEN PLAYING POKER SINCE THE EARLY 1980S. HE HOLDS THE RECORD FOR MOST WSOP VICTORIES IN EVERY DISCIPLINE. HE'S AN ECLECTIC PLAYER WHO'S A PURE GENIUS, PROBABLY ONE OF THE MOST WELL-ROUNDED PLAYERS IN THE WORLD.

"THE ORIENTAL EXPRESS"
Johnny Chan's nickname—"the Oriental Express"—was given to him when he eliminated thirteen of his fifteen opponents in thirty minutes at Bob Stupak's America's Cup of Poker. Tournament.

At a very young age, he was already doubling his salary by playing at tables where everyone was older than him. He was also on the brink of being ousted from his regular game. This is what happens when you win too often . . .

At sixteen, underage, he went to Las Vegas and sat down at a five hundred dollar table. He left the first night with twenty thousand dollars. The second night, he lost everything. Disgusted, he returned to Houston, where he stayed two years before going back to Vegas. He sold everything he had in order to leave with the most cash possible.

His winnings were mediocre. Then he stopped smoking four packs of cigarettes a day and changed both his diet and the style of his game. He became world champion at the WSOP in 1987 and 1988.

"NOT TOO MANY PLAYERS TRY TO BLUFF ME. IF THERE'S ANY BLUFFING OR STEALING, I'M GOING TO BE THE ONE TO DO IT."

DANIEL NEGREANU

CANADA'S DANIEL NEGREANU IS ONE OF THE MOST POPULAR PLAYERS IN THE UNITED STATES. A CAMERA MAGNET, NEGREANU ALWAYS HAS SOMETHING INTERESTING TO SAY AT A POKER TABLE. HE'S CONSISTENTLY IN A GOOD MOOD, RESPECTS HIS OPPONENTS, AND LOVES A CHAOTIC GAME.

Yet, his start in top-level poker wasn't easy. He learned to play in an illegal club in Toronto. For many years, he traveled around the United States, going from city to city and poker club to poker club to test his skills. This is how he acquired so much experience in so little time.

After losing his winnings in minor games, he began 2004 with strong resolutions. That year, he pocketed more than four million dollars and also won the Player of the Year trophy from the magazine *Card Player*.

"KID POKER"
Daniel "Kid Poker" Negreanu gladly recognizes that one of his strong points is his ability to decipher his opponents. He never hesitates forcing a weak hand, like a 5-2, to the flop if he knows it is a way to take a lot of chips off his opponent.

IN 2005, DANIEL NEGREANU CHALLENGED PLAYERS TO HEAD-TO-HEAD POKER, WITH STAKES AT A HUNDRED THOUSAND AND THREE HUNDRED THOUSAND DOLLARS PER GAME.

A 7 4

GUS HANSEN

GUS HANSEN, A DANE BORN IN 1974, IS FAMOUS FOR BEING THE FOUR-TIME WINNER OF THE WPT IN ITS FIRST THREE SEASONS, A RECORD THAT IS SURE TO REMAIN UNMATCHED FOR A LONG TIME. BUT HE'S ESPECIALLY KNOWN FOR THE WAY HE WON THEM, WHICH SAYS A LOT ABOUT HIS CHARACTER.

"THE GREAT DANE"
Gus "the Great Dane" Hansen will raise with any kind of hand, even strong ones. He is, par excellence, the player who plays his opponents and not his cards. It's to the point that the expression "having a Gus" means having a "garbage hand:" for example, 7-4, 10-3, 8-5, 5-2.

A great part of Hansen's strength resides in his image of being an extremely aggressive player. Because he's likely to play any cards, he makes his opponents crazy. They can't "read" him. At any moment, he could corner the attacker.

Hansen hasn't always been a poker player. He's a backgammon champion and a former junior tennis champion, too. He became a professional poker player in 1997, after discovering the game in 1993, while studying in California.

"THERE'S DEFINITELY RATIONALE BEHIND A LOT OF THINGS I DO. THEY MIGHT SEEM WACKY, BUT I'M NOT TOTALLY CRAZY, JUST A LITTLE BIT."

CHRIS FERGUSON

BORN IS 1963, CHRIS FERGUSON CAME INTO THE PUBLIC EYE AFTER HIS FAMOUS VICTORY DURING THE WSOP CHAMPIONSHIPS IN 2000. HE'S IMMEDIATELY RECOGNIZABLE. HE'S THE PLAYER WEARING THE BLACK SUNGLASSES, THE BIG STETSON HAT, AND THE BEARD THAT GAVE HIM THE NICKNAME "JESUS."

Having a university education, he left UCLA in 1999 to devote himself to top-level poker. He had been dabbling in tournaments since 1994, and participated in the WSOP irregularly since 1995. His victory in 2000 will go down in history. He was up against an experienced champion, T. J. Cloutier. Chris had A-9 and T. J. had A-Q. The board started with 2-K-4-K, and both were all-in. The river meant they could share the pot, but luck would have it otherwise: it was a 9 and Chris became world champion.

"JESUS"
Chris "Jesus" Ferguson is renowned for his sophisticated strategy articles on the mathematical aspects of the game. He brings a breath of fresh air to poker theory as well as to the simple, effective principles that have turned him into a respected player. His many victories in major tournaments have only strengthened his image.

"IF YOU'RE HESITATING BETWEEN CALLING AND RAISING, RAISE."

A♦ 7♣ 8♥

Cards on the table

THE SEVEN
ESSENTIAL RULES
OF POKER

To win at No Limit Texas Hold 'em, you have to strategize, calculate your actions, and attack at the right moment.
Here are seven rules. Memorize them. They will help you make the most out of your hand.

A FEW REMINDERS

Poker is a money game.

Always play at your financial level. If you do well at a certain price-level, don't change it. If you chose to play at more expensive tables and you stop winning, go back down. Money you earn from your job should not go to poker. You should draw your playing cash from your entertainment budget. Manage your playing cash. If it disappears, save up your funds month after month, based on your entertainment budget. It'll be an opportunity to take a break and breathe some air that doesn't smell of poker.

If you don't have an entertainment budget, don't play poker.

Play against players who are better than you.

If you only play against mediocre players, you'll certainly win, but you won't improve. The better you get at poker, the more you'll beat your various opponents at higher levels.

Playing against better players also means you'll probably lose for a while. Think of this time as a learning period. It's part of the improvement process that every serious player undergoes.

Seek excellence.

In poker, as with any activity, seek to improve. Poker can reveal entire facets of your personality you never knew existed. You might prove to be a real "killer," when you're usually very friendly. Or, you might prove to be a fearsome strategist, filled with patience, when, in your social life, you're chaotic.

Good poker players are always wise. A good part of this wisdom comes from poker.

CHOOSE
STARTIN
HAND

YOUR
G
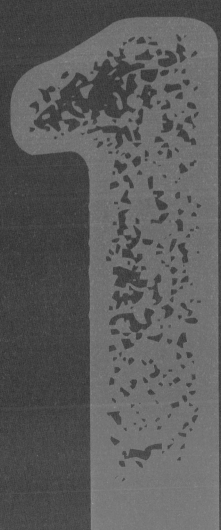

Your first decision is whether you'll enter the hand or not. There are four main factors to take into consideration:

> your stack
> your position
> your opponents (quantity and quality)
> your cards

If you don't have experience compensating for weak cards with an aggressive attitude, the decisive factor before the flop will be the quality of your hand.

IN GENERAL

- The farther you are from the button, the more you can let yourself enter with a weak hand. You can compensate for the potential weakness with the information you cull from being in late position.
- The fewer opponents you have at the table, the more you can let yourself enter with a weak hand. When the field is reduced, the probability of being dealt a specific type of hand is still the same, but the probability of coming up against strong hands lessens, and therefore the average value of a hand improves.
- The more chips you have in comparison to your opponent, the more you can intimidate him by attacking or calling him.

HIGH HANDS:
A-A, K-K, Q-Q, A-K

When you have a strong hand, it's ideal to face only one opponent on the flop. When you have multiple opponents, if a straight draw or flush draw flops, one of your opponents may have a strong draw. Attack and raise preflop to narrow the field and drive out speculative hands.

POTENTIAL HANDS:
A PAIR INFERIOR
TO A PAIR OF JACKS

As opposed to high hands, the player has to play a potential hand against the greatest number of opponents possible and bet the lowest possible amount.

A player holding a pair, no matter the rank, will flop trips (three of a kind) roughly one out of nine times. That's not often. But when a player flops a set, the hand will be so strong and so unexpected that, most every time, it will win a big pot.

General attitude: because your middle or low pair is unlikely to be an overpair on the flop, it's best to see the flop cheaply and hope to flop three of a kind. Because this doesn't happen often, you should be able to see the flop without it costing you too much. That is, of course, if there are several opponents to fatten up the pot.

POTENTIAL HANDS: A FLUSH DRAW

A flush draw is A-x or K-x, suited: for example, A♠-8♠, K♥-5♥. These hands should only be played by experienced players; that is, by players who can accurately evaluate their chance of winning the hand. These hands flop a flush draw roughly one out of eight times. They flop a high hand, like two pair, a three of a kind, or even a straight, also one out of eight times. The rest of the time—that is, six times out of eight—they're pretty bad off.

POTENTIAL HANDS: SUITED CONNECTORS

Suited connectors are two cards that are consecutive in rank and of the same suit: J♠-10♠, 10♥-9♥, 9♣-8♣. Even more than a flush draw, suited connectors will rarely improve your hand. You need experience with them. Fold even if you have a big hand.

The advantage of suited connectors is that they improve on the flop one out of two times, flopping a pair, two pair, straight, flush, three of a kind, full house, or four of a kind.

In these dangerous situations, on the flop, the only valid strategy is to attack the pot and try to win it right away. But, don't call the opponent's raise.

Note: a flush draw is more easily read by your opponents than a straight draw.

CONCLUSION

If you follow these rules, you'll enter the hand about 21 percent of the time.

The following will increase this rate:
- If you're the big blind and if no one raises you, you'll see the flop no matter what your hand is.
- If you're in a good position and playing against adequate players, varying your way of playing could let you play hands your opponent won't expect, like a suited 7-5 or a Q-10, for example. These actions are essential, but should not be played regularly.
- If you're at the end of a tournament, especially heads-up, you should enter hands more often.

The following will decrease this rate:
- If you don't have a lot of experience, you should limit playing delicate hands like suited connectors, perhaps avoiding it completely.
- The anxiety of playing in a very tight hand in a tense and long tournament may contribute to decreasing the rate.

PREFLOP

Antes: $5,000 - Blinds: $20,000–$40,000

Gus Hansen in seat 4 raises to $110,000 with J♦-J♣.
Abe Mosseri, the small blind, calls with A♥-J♥.
After the first betting round, the pot contains $290,000.

With the pair of jacks he has been dealt, Hansen raises to reduce the field. Mosseri decides to call with his suited ace jack.

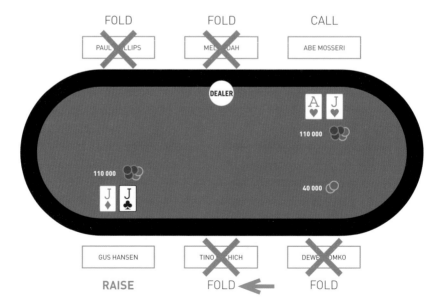

FLOP
Q♠-4♠-3♥

Mosseri has nothing on the flop and checks.
Hansen doesn't want to take the risk of Mosseri check-raising
him on the queen-high flop, so he also checks.

TURN
4♥

The four on the turn doesn't help anyone, because Mosseri could not
have called preflop with a hand that included a four, unless it were A-5
or 5-4.

But Mosseri doesn't try to steal the pot and checks again.
Hansen checks as well.

CALL THE RIVER
3♣

The river doesn't help anyone, except now the board has two pair, fours, and threes.

From this point of view, Mosseri isn't so bad off, because his ace improves the board.

Instead of attacking, Mosseri mulls it over, then decides to check.

Now Hansen can only believe he has the best hand. Because of the action, it's unlikely that Mosseri has a queen, a three, or a four. **Hansen decides to bet $100,000.**

Mosseri is amazed and asks, "What are you thinking, Gus?" Hansen remains unshakable and mechanically counts his chips.

Mosseri finally decides to call the $100,000.
Hansen shows the winning hand.

WHY DID MOSSERI CALL THE RIVER?

The pot had $390,000. It cost $100,000 to call. The pot odds were four to one. But was he getting the right odds to make this call? Hansen is known to raise preflop with low cards, so he could very well have had a three or a four, maybe a low pair other than 2-2. Even a borderline hand like Q-8 would have been enough to beat Mosseri.

Because Mosseri could not put Hansen on a better hand, he called to show his two pair with the ace kicker. Unless Hansen was bluffing, the only hand Mosseri could beat was king high.

Mosseri lost because he couldn't accept that he was being bluffed by a bluff pro. Only the best players can stop themselves from falling into this trap. Those who can't have little chance of winning a big tournament.

ODDS

In poker, odds are a rational way to make a decision. There are two factors at play: the probability of winning and the financial payback of the hand. If a hand that wins one out of three times brings in as much as what you bet, the danger is worth it and the risk should be taken. If it brings in three times what you bet, the danger is well worth it and it would be a mistake not to take the risk. Players who ignore the idea of odds commit two kinds of diametrically opposed mistakes: they run a risk they should avoid, and they avoid a risk they should take.

ATTACK
A MEANS
PROTECT

AS
OF
ION

2

The more you attack, the fewer opponents you'll have, and the more chance you'll have of winning the hand, because the field is reduced. You clearly have more chance of winning a one-on-one fight than a one-on-four fight. Attacking, therefore, protects you.

THE IDEA
OF A JUMBO
RERAISE

In order to "break the opponent's odds" (see "Glossary," pages TK), that is, in order to mathematically dissuade players from calling your raise, your raise has to be strong. If your usual preflop raise is four times the big blind, increase your raise by an amount equal to one big blind for every player who has called the big blind. For example: you're the button, and three players have already called the big blind. Your jumbo reraise will therefore be 4 + 3 = 7 times the big blind. If the big blind is 100, you should bet 700.

CHRIS FERGUSON
AND THE PRINCIPLE
OF BEING AGGRESSIVE

Chris "Jesus" Ferguson was world champion in 2000. He's a precise and aggressive player. Here are his two laws of being aggressive.

FERGUSON'S FIRST LAW
OF BEING AGGRESSIVE

"If you're the first to act, you never call. Instead, raise or fold."

This goes for the UTG player or anyone opening the action.

This rule will teach the player two things: how to put pressure on his opponents and how to make clear-cut decisions. At first glance, this law seems strange. But it isn't. When strictly followed, it will turn you into a cold, respected, and aggressive player. You'll come off as dangerous.

FERGUSON'S LAW OF BEING AGGRESSIVE

"If you're choosing between calling and folding, fold."

"If you're choosing between calling and raising, raise."

"If you're choosing between folding and raising, think."

This law prevents limping except in these rare cases:
- preflop, with a good potential hand, like Jh-Th, if several players have already entered the hand;
- on the flop or after, with a huge hand, like four of a kind, to push an opponent to stealing the pot.

DON'T GIVE YOUR OPPONENT A FREE CARD

If you're the first to act and check, you're leaving the hand open to your opponent. If he has an average hand, he'll be tempted to bet and attack. If he has a draw, he can check and take a free card, which could make a straight or a flush. If you bet right away, you'll pull the rug out from under him. He'll only be able to call you if he has a big hand.

ONE EXCEPTION: THE CHECK AND RAISE

If you check, and if your opponent bets, you'll check-raise if you decide to raise him. The check-raise is one of the most powerful attacks in No Limit Hold 'em. It gives your opponent a chance to bluff at the pot, when he would have folded had you bet out, earning you the chips he bluffed.

To call a check-raise, a player has to have an excellent hand. If some players call with a draw to see the following card (turn), and if the turn is unfavorable, they then won't be able to continue in the hand.

THE CONTINUATION BET

When a player has attacked or counterattacked preflop, it's in his every interest to continue his attack on the flop. In this situation, he has an additional chance of winning the hand immediately if his opponent feels weak.

DON'T GIVE AN AGGRESSIVE PLAYER ANY ELBOW ROOM

If you don't attack first, your opponent probably will. By keeping the pressure on your opponent, you'll make him panic. You'll paralyze him. His only choice is to fold. When you've found a player who loses his cool easily when attacked, make sure to attack first.

But avoid attacking solid players who aren't easily fooled.

POKER CEMETERIES ARE FILLED WITH OVERLY AGGRESSIVE PLAYERS

An overly aggressive player, or a player who is aggressive too often, runs the risk of finding himself trapped when he's up against a very high hand. An aggressive player must, therefore, be able to detect the dangerous moment. He should be able to either fold easily or raise as soon as he feels he's in danger.

PREFLOP

Blinds: $25-50 - Stack: $10,000 for each player

Erick Lindgren (seat 4) limps in with 3♣-3♠.
Players 5 and 6 call.
Small blind calls.
T. J. Cloutier (big blind) checks with A♥-6♥.

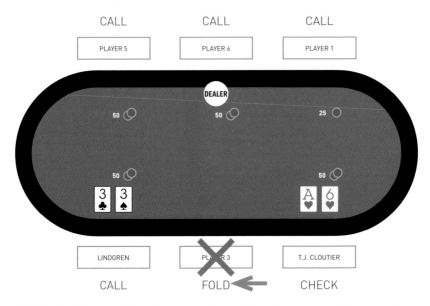

It's the first hand of the tournament and the players aren't warmed up yet. Cloutier seizes the opportunity to see the flop and to potentially play the odds. Lindgren is in the same situation: he has a low pair and there's no point in raising preflop, especially in early position. The pot has $250.

FLOP
Q♥-10♥-3♥

Cloutier flops a flush and Lindgren hits a set.

The small blind checks and Cloutier also chooses to check. Lindgren does not want to let a player with a bare heart draw for free and decides to bet.

Then something unusual happens for this level of competition. Lindgen may have felt thrown off-kilter by such a strong hand in the first round. He confuses the chips when raising. Or he forgets that the pot isn't $2,500 but $250. The fact is that instead of betting $220, he bets $2,200.

The other players fold, except for Cloutier, who decides to call.

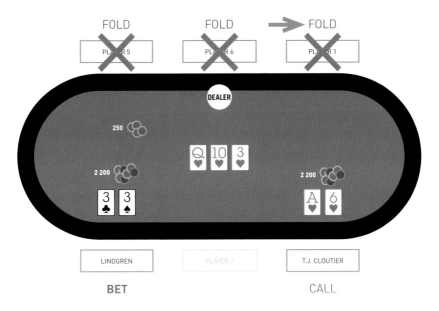

The pot is $4,650.

TURN
Q♠

The queen paired the board and made Lindgren threes full of queens. This is a terrible card for Cloutier if he puts Lindgren on trip queens, because he can beat trip queens. At this point, Cloutier has already lost the hand, but he doesn't know it. He even thinks he's won.

Cloutier logically decides to bet. But instead of betting a typical amount, around $3,000, for example, he bets $6,500 at a pot that only has $4,650.

Why such a high bet? If Lindgren does, in fact, have trip queens, the bet is obviously not going to stop him from raising Cloutier all-in.

And that's exactly what Lindgren does: he raises all-in immediately to $7,750, hoping Cloutier has a flush and will call.

Cloutier knows a full house beats his flush. But Lindgren could also only have a three of a kind. In any case, he only has $1,200 left and the pot is $19,000.

Cloutier doesn't hesitate. He calls.

There's a showdown and Cloutier leaves the table immediately. The story doesn't reveal what the river was, but in any case, it doesn't change a thing, because Cloutier had already lost.

CONCLUSION

Cloutier is in an ideal position to apply Chris Ferguson's principle: in raising the big blind to about $400, he would have made what is called a "squeeze play," and would have probably won the pot, taking in a profit of $200. And if someone had called, he could have protected his flush . . . and this someone would probably not have been Lindgren who, coming right after Cloutier, would not have had the odds to call with two miserable threes.

VARY YO
WAY OF
PLAYING

All great champions know that figuring out how their opponent plays is key to winning. An opponent who's easy to figure out will be easy to attack: you just have to avoid him when he's going strong and go for the kill when he's bluffing. You also have to hope your opponent won't do the same. The key, therefore, is to give false signals and confuse your opponent in order to lead him astray. **The most direct way to accomplish this is to vary your way of playing.**

MISTAKE NUMBER ONE: ESTABLISHING A LINE OF CONDUCT AND NEVER STRAYING FROM IT

If a player is too strict about his actions, he's bound to meet his "death" because he'll become obvious to his opponent. A player who can be read too easily will react mostly the same way to similar situations: he'll always attack the same way, with the same cards, under the same circumstances.

An experienced opponent loves this kind of player for two reasons:

1. Because the experienced player can easily guess what his opponent has, he'll know how to step out of the hand as soon as the opponent enters it. For example, if an apprehensive player in early position raises preflop, his alert opponents will know he has a very high hand: A-A, K-K, A-K, or Q-Q.

2. Every cold-footed player in the world folds out of fear of calling a hand he's already lost. An experienced player will attack this player, because he knows he won't call the raise.

MISTAKE NUMBER TWO: UNDERESTIMATING YOUR OPPONENTS

When a player doesn't vary his game, it means he thinks his opponents are inexperienced. He thinks his way of playing is all he needs to beat them.

But in no limit poker, with eight or nine very different opponents at the table, the hand categories you'll face will always be different.

This means you must attempt two things:

1. Try to categorize each player and create a profile.
2. Adapt your game to each profile.

If you don't enter a hand, which is basically eight out of ten hands, you should take that time to watch other players and absorb as much information as you can.

"Seventy percent of the win depends on your ability to observe your opponent," says Phil Hellmuth, world champion in 1989.

In varying your game, you'll throw experienced players off track when they try to size you up. They'll have a lot of trouble categorizing you and will avoid a head-to-head showdown. Consequently, you'll mostly face weak or predictable players, who are much easier to beat.

HOW TO PROCEED CONCRETELY

First, you need to be an aggressive player. This should be your core profile. If no one knows you at the table, it's always better to come off as an apprehensive or "mouse" player.

Then, a half hour or an hour later, change gears: attack often. Follow Ferguson's law and raise preflop every time you're the first player after the big blind. This kind of attack isn't expensive and will give you an out if there's a counterattack, unless you have a high hand, of course.

When you change tables, change your profile. Become a "caller," a "calling station," or an "elephant." The advantage is, when your draw improves on the turn, your simple bet will make your opponent fold. In another half hour or so, go back to a winning strategy: be an aggressive player.

Varying your game also means playing the opposite way you're used to, about one out of five hands. Because your core game is the attack, this means entering the pot with a good potential hand without raising. Opponents will think you're slacking off or tired. They'll think you're "on tilt."

Sometimes, make the mistake of showing your cards even though you don't have to. Do it simply to show you stayed in with a potential hand against an aggressive player.

Change your moods. Be unpredictable and alternate from being silent to annoyed to talkative.

Warning: never try to come off as eccentric, because an experienced player will always be able to corner you. Instead of betting moderately to draw attention, try instead to come off as dangerous, capable of going all-in with a pair of aces on the flop.

Good players always fear players who counterattack extravagantly: are they bluffing or are they trying to get my stack? Unless he has the best hand, a good player will most often fold in this situation.

PREFLOP
Blinds: $1,500–$3,000

Mike Matusow ($394,000) raises to $12,000 with 9♠-7♠.
Greg Raymer ($277,000) reraises to $36,000 with A♦-J♦.
Matusow calls.

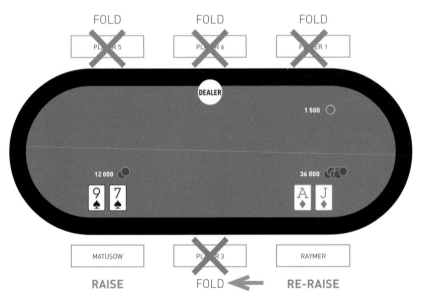

FLOP

Raymer goes all-in.

It's a classic semi-bluff but huge because he bets three times the pot.
Matusow mulls it over. He could be behind if Raymer has 10-x, but he
thinks that his opponent has A-K or A-Q instead. Therefore, he thinks
his pair of nines is good.

CALL

Matusow ends up calling.

TURN

This is the worst card for Matusow because it gives his opponent the nut flush. His opponent has therefore won the hand.

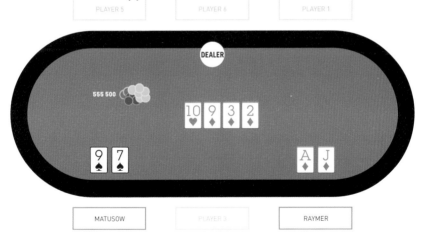

CONCLUSION

Here, against Raymer who's on a roll, Matusow has read his opponent correctly. He calls with the second pair, because he "feels" he has the advantage. Matusow proves here that he can rely on his intuition. It's a quality that serves him well at tournaments.

PREFLOP

Blinds: $1,500–$3,000

Matusow (two off the button) calls with 10♦-10♣.
Raymer (big blind) checks with A♣-9♣.

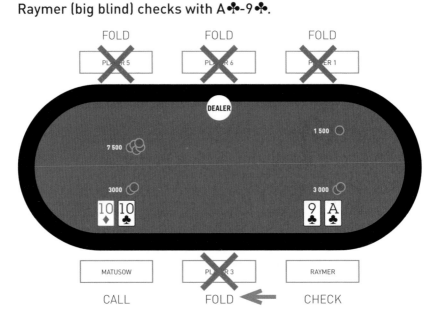

FLOP

Q♠-6♣-3♠

The flop doesn't help either player.
Raymer checks, ready to fold to any bet.
Matusow checks behind.

TURN
K♠

Raymer checks by tapping the table.
Matusow checks again.

You would have expected Matusow to be more lively and ready to bet here. But he does nothing, as if he were surrendering.

RIVER
A♠

Raymer checks again.
Matusow could try to steal the pot by betting and making his opponent believe he has a spade flush. But he also checks.

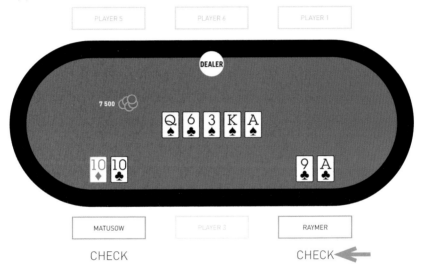

At the showdown, it's obviously Raymer who wins because of the ace he caught on the river.

CONCLUSION

These two hands show how a big player can vary his game. In the preceding hand, Matusow was really aggressive. This time, against the same opponent, he waits and sees, as if he were expecting his opponent to attempt a bluff, which never happened.

TAKE ADV
OF YOUR
OPPONEN
WEAKNES

Poker is a game of confrontation: if you win, it's not that you're categorically good, it's that you're better than your opponent. Playing at a table with only big-time professionals when you're not one suggests you rely only on luck to win. Don't count on luck; everyone has the same amount of it.

In the long term, you'll stand out because of your strategy and attitude.

REGULAR OBSERVATION OF YOUR OPPONENTS ALLOWS YOU TO BETTER UNDERSTAND THEIR WEAKNESSES

Regular observation will help you adapt your game.

The core method of adaptation is to take the opposite course. For example:

- If you're at an overly tight table, go ahead and take risks, play loose. Your bluffs will rarely be called, and if the reraiser has a big hand, you can fold without regretting it, because he's sure to have a strong hand.

- If you're at an overly loose table, play tight. You'll let your opponents take senseless risks and you'll only enter the hand if you have better-than-average cards.

The following is a list of different types of players and how your power of adaptation and observation can help exploit your opponents' every weakness.

A Player Who Isn't 100 Percent

A player who is tired, sick, out of breath, a bit drunk, or jet-lagged, isn't 100 percent on. Take advantage of this handicap.

A Readable Player

Some players are predictable: they always react the same way when facing an aggressive player or when they're attacking themselves.

A Broke Player

A broke player feels compelled to win the hand. This means he'll makes the basic mistake of playing in order not to lose. But in order to play well, your mind has to be free. Experienced opponents will notice it. They're more likely to bluff a conservative player.

A Rich Player

A rich player doesn't have the same weaknesses as a broke player, but he does have weaknesses. The advantage he has is that he can create a game budget. But, oddly, only some rich players have one. Most couldn't care less. Those are the best kind of rich players to pit yourself against. Because they spend carelessly, they'll do the same in poker. Result: they gamble huge sums of money to call to see another card even if they don't have the odds. Take advantage of this extravagant behavior.

A Rushed Player

Time is money. No one knows this better than a player who's in a hurry. He's not going to wait for the optimal situation to bet: good cards, position, stack, or opponents. Therefore, he'll play more often than he should and at times that aren't right. Inevitably, he's more vulnerable.

An On-Edge Player

It's easy to spot a player who is on edge: he throws his cards down violently when he loses, he reacts strongly, he sighs . . . all signs of a player struggling with luck, which he thinks he can control. This kind of player isn't clearheaded enough to face an experienced player who's just waiting for an excellent hand to trap him.

An Inexperienced Player

You won't get the better of an inexperienced player easily because:
- He doesn't know what "the odds" are. Because he might draw to a flush when he's not getting the right price, don't try to "break his odds" with a raise.
- He doesn't understand the nuances of a bluff. Therefore, don't bluff as much against him.
- He doesn't understand the subtleties of a "false tell." His actions or signs are bound to lead to a mistake.
- Reraises, all-ins, and sometimes check-raises impress him. So be aggressive.

- He clumsily tries to make you think he has a different hand than he does. So be aware.

A Big Pro

Big professionals can be beat, even though they've mastered the finer aspects of the game. They're especially dangerous for opponents who haven't: they know their odds, they check-raise fearlessly, they reraise, etc. Although he comes off as aggressive, he's actually prudent.

If a professional player is aggressive, avoid being overly aggressive: on the contrary, call him. And if he's holding back, attack. Alternate between these two attitudes, because a great player is a chameleon: he constantly changes technique. Don't count on throwing him off course. To win against this kind of player, you have to use certain subtle bluffs. Don't be unwilling to lead him down the wrong track.

PREFLOP
Antes: $1,000 - Blinds: $5,000–$10,000

Matusow (button) calls the big blind with K♥-2♥.
Negreanu (small blind) calls with 8♥-7♠.
Sexton (big blind) checks with 7♣-3♠.

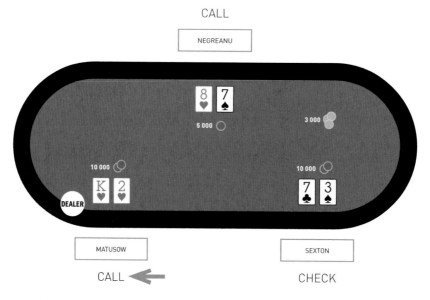

Pot: $33,000.

FLOP
Q♥-9♠-3♥

This flop gives Matusow a flush draw, a pair of Threes for Sexton, and nothing for Negreanu.

Negreanu checks.
Sexton checks.
Matusow checks.

It's amazing that Matusow checks because he's an aggressive player who is used to semi-bluffing hands when he's got position, which is the case here. He flopped the second nut-flush draw, and yet doesn't make a play at the pot.

TURN
A♣

Negreau checks.
Sexton checks.
Matusown bets $20K, which is two-thirds of the pot.
Negreanu folds.
Sexton calls.

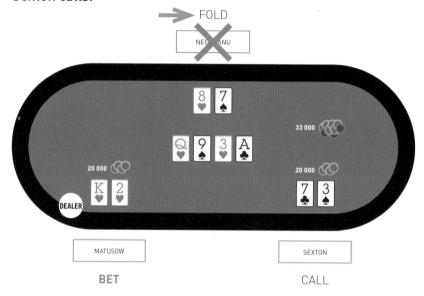

RIVER
J♦

Sexton checks.
Matusow bets $60K, which is 80 percent of the pot.
Sexton calls.

Feeling the chill of death, Matusow shows his king high Sexton shows his pair of threes and wins.

CONCLUSION

How does Sexton have the presence of mind to call when the only hands he can beat are a missed flush draw in hearts or a pure bluff? Is he clairvoyant? If he calls his opponent, it's because he felt his opponent's weakness in the three previous stages of the hand:
- Matusow's last bet, 80 percent of the pot, proves he doesn't have a strong hand. If the Jack gave him a straight, he would have bet $25K or $35K so that Sexton would have called or been forced to raise. He also couldn't have a pair of jacks because he would have never bet and would have also chosen to check and go to the showdown.
- On the turn, the ace froze Matusow, and Sexton saw that it did. Matusow therefore could not have a pair of aces.
- On the flop, Matusow, who acts last, can try to steal the pot without difficulty. If he doesn't do it, it's because he doesn't have a pair of queens . . . and probably not a pair of nines, either.
In the end, what could Matusow have? A pair of nines, a pair of threes, a missed flush draw, or nothing at all. Sexton tells himself the odds are on his side with his Threes. Therefore, he calls and wins. Matusow must have regretted not having raised preflop. Even if he only won the blinds, he would have at least won this hand, because no one would have called.

BLUFF
CAREFUL

LY

5

There's no poker without bluffing. Without bluffing, there's no winner either. A tournament winner is always someone who has bluffed at some point or other during the event.

Bluffs are when a player attacks without a hand, in hopes that the opponent will fold. Obviously, a bluffer only wants to bluff when he knows he's not the favorite, and when he feels his opponent isn't the favorite, either. (If the bluffer's opponent is the favorite, he'll call the bluff, maybe even raise, and the bluffer will have no choice but fold.)

THERE ARE SEVERAL KINDS OF BLUFFS

The Semi-Bluff

This means bluffing with a potential hand, even with a hand that might already be a winning one.

For example, you have T-9 and the flop is A-J-8. Now you have a straight draw. If a player bets before you and if another calls him, raising will be profitable for you. That said, you'll have two chances of winning the hand:

1. immediately, if no one calls your raise;

2. after, if the card on the turn or the river is an "out"; that is, in this case, a seven or a queen.

The Pure-Bluff

There's no way out of a pure bluff. No card will improve your hand. The pure bluffer isn't playing his cards. He's playing his position, his stack, and the personality of his opponents.

If the bluffer feels that by raising at that precise moment, his opponent won't call, he should raise, no matter what kind of hand he has. It would even be a mistake not to. This way, he'll be the only one left in the hand and will automatically win the pot without showing his cards.

Slow-Play

Slow-playing, or trapping, involves playing weakly, or overplaying, when, in fact, you have a huge hand. The goal is to force the opponent to bluff, which he'll do in order to steal the pot or give him a chance to improve his hand. If it improves, he'll raise, not knowing he's already lost.

The Oak Bluff

You attempt an oak bluff when you have a very big hand and feel that your opponent is weak. Instead of betting a usual amount, bet very low. This lures your opponent into calling, certainly without hope. You'll get a few extra chips from him, which may make a difference when the time comes. You can also oak bluff when you have a very weak hand and you're playing against an experienced player. The experienced player will see an "oak play" and will hesitate before calling.

COMMON MISTAKES WHEN BLUFFING

Bluffing Too Often

Wanting to emulate the champions on TV, most inexperienced players bluff too often. But televised tournaments don't show every hand. They only show a selection of spectacular hands, which often involve bluffs. How often should you bluff? There's no norm; it'll depend on various factors, the most important being your own temperament. One out of ten hands played is a good average.

Bluffing Anyone and Everyone

Always bluff a particular player, except preflop when, for example, the blind or the big blind raises to steal the stakes ("squeeze play"). It's a mistake to bluff a beginner, an extravagant player, or a player with a lot of chips, as they'll tend to call the raise. It's better to bluff players who generally don't call the raise: conservative players and players who don't have a lot of chips, for example.

Bluffing Any Old Way

Bluffing is a strategic weapon. You don't bluff because you feel like it. You bluff when it's the right moment and because you stand to win a big pot. A player who bluffs for the thrill of it is making a mistake and will lose in the long run.

Bluffing without a Financial Payoff

There's no point bluffing for a small pot. The bluff in general and the counterattack in particular is only worth it if the pot is fat.

Bluffing without Conviction or Believability

There's nothing worse than improvising a bluff. A bluff has to be coherent. Your opponent, if he's experienced, will review every one of your actions from the beginning of the hand. If you're not being coherent, he'll call the bluff. The bluff an opponent has the least chance of calling is a believable one, played exactly as if the player has the hand he wants to make you think he has.

Refusing to Be Bluffed

There are bluffers who never get called and there are players who always call bluffers; that is, until they call a player who really has a big hand. Take a player who raises you all-in at a crucial moment of the tournament. If you have an average hand and if nothing tells you how good his hand is, you should accept that you're being bluffed. You'll be wrong one out of ten times, but nine out of ten times you'll be right, which is enough. Being bluffed is never a big deal if it lets you continue in the tournament with a big-enough stack.

PREFLOP
Blinds: $2,500–$5,000

David Angel, seat six, raises to $20,000 with A♠-10♠.
Mattias Andersson, small blind, calls the raise with 6♣-6♦.
Dan Harrington, big blind, calls the raise 9♣-9♦.

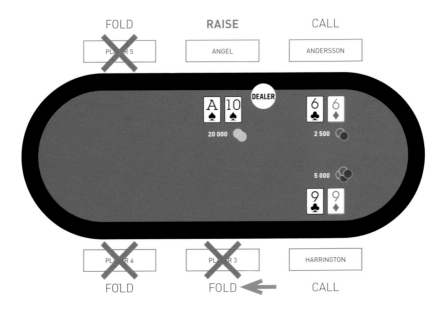

FLOP
9♥-2♠-2♥

The flop is ideal for Harrington since it gives him the top full house and a potential flush draw for an opponent.

Andersson bets $40,000.
Harrington smooth-calls.

Above all, Harrington doesn't want to scare the following player, who could also raise. It proves pointless, because Angel folds and lets the two other players finish the hand together. The challenge for Harrington is to get the greatest number of chips possible from his opponent.

TURN
K♥

This third heart is exactly the card Harrington was waiting for. And Andersson wants to keep the pressure on his opponent by making him believe he has a flush.

Andersson bets $70,000.
Harrington again smooth-calls, as if he were hesitating.
He continues to set the trap.

RIVER
3♣

Because the last card doesn't change anything, it pushes Andersson to try to take over the hand and continue with his lead as if he had two hearts or a two in his hand against Harrington, with a Nine.

Andersson bets $70,000 again.
Harrington pretends to hesitate, then raises the lowest possible amount, to $150,000.

Andersson mulls it over before doing the only reasonable thing: he folds.

CONCLUSION

This kind of bluff is rare, because the hand really rests on chance. Harrington has every advantage: first, his hand, then his position, and also the fact that he's an aggressive player.

Strangely enough, this ideal situation is extremely stressful for the player. It's not that defeat is possible, but, on the contrary, that there's an obligation to keep the opponent in the hand in order to collect the maximum number of chips.

No one could possibly blame Andersson for his steady attack, even though Harrington's call on the flop should have set off a warning bell against betting the turn. In any case, this is what a conservative player would have done. But Andersson is of a different ilk, especially when his stack lets him be so.

ACCEPT YOU WILL BLUFFED

The worst mistake in No Limit Texas Hold 'em is sticking to your cards. And, in general, sticking to a situation when it's clear you're not going to win or when you know your opponent went all-in to intimidate you. In this case, it's your ego that's on the line. And a player obsessed with his ego will never win a tournament.

EGO AND PANACHE

In poker, ego is counterproductive. Panache is outdated. It means winning or losing magnificently. Unfortunately, it's rarely awarded in poker, at least never in a defensive situation. Panache that pays in poker is called an attack.

For example, a player who raises preflop with 7-4 runs a huge risk. But because he's attacking, the risk is greatly reduced. If this player, furthermore, has a lot of chips, if he's the button, and if the previous raiser is an apprehensive player who rarely calls or reraises, it's easy to understand why the player attacked: he's banking on the fact that his opponent will fold and leave him the pot.

The idea is to attack when you have the best chance of winning the hand. The reraiser with a 7-4 hand is not in the right situation, but he compensates with the advantages his stack and position offer him.

By attacking, he gives himself two chances to win:
1. The opponent folds right away and the pot goes to the aggressive player.
2. The opponent calls and the flop could improve the hand.

But, just like in tennis, where a player could return the ball twice as hard, a poker opponent could himself reraise. In this case, because he has no strong cards, the aggressive player better fold right away: he knows his opponent has a very good hand and that he'll "stick" for the rest of the hand.

DEFENSIVE PANACHE

Defensive panache is something else entirely. If with an average hand, like 8-8, for example, you decide to call preflop, you know that an eight on the flop will give you a great hand. But you also know that without this eight (which you only have one in nine chance of getting), you should find a different strategy.

This other solution is knowing for certain that the opponent is bluffing. You might call to try to see his cards because you feel compelled to know if he's bluffing or not. And bluffing someone like you means he's taking you for an idiot. That's too much.

MENTAL TORTURE
AND RABBIT HUNTING

You have to accept that folding to a bully means you're never going to know your opponent's hand. It's hard to pass up knowing if your opponent did or did not have a good hand. You have to be able to let go. When the pot has been won, another hand begins.

If you've been playing a while, you've certainly already seen people rabbit hunt. At the end of the hand, because they've decided to fold, they ask to see the cards that would have been in play "if they had continued playing." This doesn't change a thing about the hand and can only bring regret . . . and ridicule.

TAKE CARE
OF YOURSELF

You have to get used to forgetting about the hand that just happened. It's sometimes hard, sometimes counterinstinctive, but you have to fight against the urge.

Instead of marrying your cards, get divorced from them as soon as you don't need them anymore. Instead of thinking your opponent is a bluffer, accept the idea that he had a very good hand.

What if he tells you he had K-K, or another other huge hand? If he doesn't show you anything, he could be telling you just about anything. What if he shows you a garbage hand? It doesn't matter. Convince yourself that if he plays the same hand ten times, he'll only bluff once and will beat you the nine other times!

PREFLOP
Antes: $1,000 - Blinds: $4,000–$8,000

Mickey Seagle folds.
Carlos Mortensen raises to $24K with J♣-9♣.
David Oppenheim reraises to $74K with 4♠-4♦.
Randy Burger, Charles Shoten, and Noli Francisco fold.

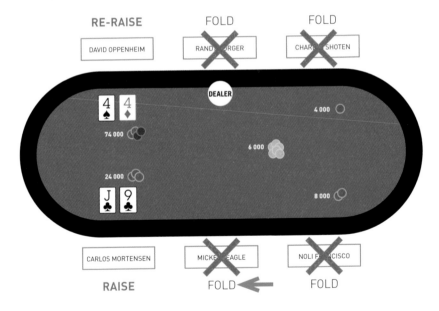

Oppenheim reraises Mortensen preflop with only 4-4. He clearly does it to take the lead in the hand and try to block the next player from reraising. Unfortunately for him, the other players fold, except for the raiser, who calls him.

Carlos Mortensen calls.

The fact that Mortensen calls here with only J-9 is speculative: he's looking for a good flop with two clubs for a flush draw or a straight draw. Calling in this situation is clearly a gamble, but Mortensen sees the opportunity for luck to do its thing.

FLOP
8♥-3♥-8♣

It's a paired flop, therefore opening the possibility of three of a kind, even a full house. Furthermore, there are two hearts, making a possible flush draw.

      Mortensen has absolutely nothing significant: no pairs, no hope of a flush, only the dim hope of a straight. His only strength: his two overcards (two cards of higher rank than any showing on the board).

Mortensen is looking for a free card and checks.

This action is arguable in that it allows his opponent to have a free card rather than to maintain pressure. Unless he wants to concede the hand, Oppenheim can't check. The only card that can help him is a Four. He, therefore, has to try to steal the pot now.

Logically, Oppenheim bets $100K.

Mortensen mulls it over for a few seconds, then doubles the bet, raising to $200K.

Mortensen probably felt his opponent was weak. By reraising, he makes Oppenheim believe that he has a strong hand. Although Mortensen has the weaker hand here, his preflop action and check-raise on the flop make Oppenheim think he's strong.

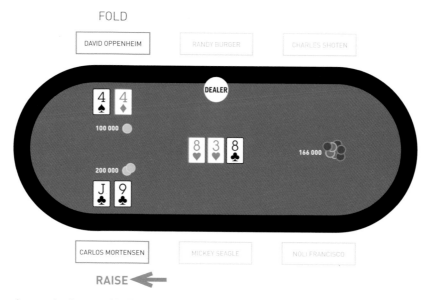

FOLD

DAVID OPPENHEIM | RANDY BURGER | CHARLES SHOTEN

DEALER

4♠ 4♦

100 000

8♥ 3♥ 8♣

166 000

200 000

J♣ 9♣

CARLOS MORTENSEN | MICKEY SEAGLE | NOLI FRANCISCO

RAISE ←

Oppenheim mulls it over for a long time, then folds.

Oppenheim can absolutely not call the reraise. Oppenheim could reraise all-in, which would make his opponent fold. But, not knowing Mortensen's full hand, he chooses to take the smart road and pulls out of the hand, donating $174K to Mortensen.

CONCLUSION

This hand shows three important lessons:
1. even when you're an aggressive player like Oppenheim, you can still fold;
2. even when you have the best of it, you can lose the hand;
3. even when you only have a low pair, you can reraise preflop.

MANAGE YOUR TOURNAM

It's no contest: a tournament is the best atmosphere for bringing out everything No Limit Texas Hold 'em has to offer. Players are forced to draw on their strategic abilities. Even without a lot of tournament experience, **you can be sure that with patience and care you'll be able to manage your tournament without too much difficulty.**

PRINCIPLES

1. Every player in the tournament pays the same amount and receives the same number of chips.

2. Bets increase regularly, about every half hour, so that players don't "play dead" while others take risks.

3. As players are eliminated, tables become more rare. At the final table, players continue to be eliminated until there is only one player left: the winner.

4. The entry fee generates the prize pool. Generally, one-tenth of the players make the money. The smallest prize covers the entry fee. The three top players share 75 percent of the total prize pool.

TOOLS FOR MANAGING YOUR TOURNAMENT

Although players might learn the game's tactics hand by hand rather fast, they nevertheless have problems managing their tournament over time.

However, when playing no limit, the smallest mistake can ruin you. Each and every player could lose his entire stack with every action. For this reason, don't ever enter a pot without conviction: it's the best way to lose your whole stack.

1. The Average Stack

The average stack is equal to the total number of chips in the tournament divided by the number of players still playing.

Always see where you stand with regard to this number:
- If your stack = average stack (within 5 percent): there's no emergency.
- If your stack < average stack or less: take risks.
- If your stack > average stack or more: don't waste your money, try some draws to eliminate a few small stacks and avoid confrontations with big stacks.

The M-Ratio

This is the number of rounds your stack can afford.

For example:
- Your stack = $10,000
- Blinds = $50–$100
- Therefore, the cost per round = $150
- And, therefore, M = $10,000 / $150 = 67

By definition:
- If M > 20: there's no emergency. You have time to wait.
- If 10 < M < 20: begin attacking every now and then.
- If 5 < M < 10: steal the blinds and take risks on the attack.
- If M < 5: only attack by going all-in.

Let Your Opponents Duke It Out

If you have a playable hand and if two opponents go all-in before you, think before joining the battle. If you have a big hand and if you have twice as many chips as your opponent, why not?

But if you are already in the money, and have a decent but unexceptional hand—a 10-10 or A-J, for example—and a smaller stack, it would clearly be better to let your opponents duel it out alone. This means you fold, as if you were escaping a bad hand.

Observe other tables

Every now and then, get up, walk around, and take mental notes. Not only will you stretch out your legs, but, above all else, you'll also be able to see if there are any threats. In locating the big stacks, you'll also spot players who are on a roll and dangerous.

Take note if there are only two or three tables left. These are your future opponents. Learn how they play and try to increase your stack to match theirs.

The Point of No-Return

All players reach this point at some time or other. This is the point when your stack has eroded to an M-ratio of 2 or 3. Because you're only as intimidating as your stack size, you absolutely have to double its size in order to continue in the tournament. As soon as you have a decent hand, one that is better than average, you have to go all-in and hope that the big stack at the table will call you with whatever hand he has. And if no one calls you, you'll win the blinds, which are always high at this point in the tournament.

PREFLOP
Blinds: $16,000–$32,000

Brandon Schaefer has 10♦-10♣ and raises $45K
Justin Bonomo has A♣-Q♣ and raises all-in to $164K.
Carl Olson calls with A♠-Q♦.
Mark Ristine folds.
Schaefer calls.

Schaefer decides not to reraise, hoping he and Olson can eliminate Bonomo. This implicit collusion improves their chances of finishing the tournament in third. This way, they both stand to earn a bigger payout.

FLOP
9♦-6♥-2♠

The flop has no draws and doesn't improve anyone's hand. Schaefer remains the favorite with his overpair (a pair whose rank is higher than that of any card on the board).

Olson checks.
Schaefer also checks.

Olson gives Schaefer the possibility of checking, too. Usually, especially heads-up, Schaefer's strategy would be to bet the pot, even go all-in. But here, the challenge is not to win the hand, but to eliminate Bonomo.

TURN
6♠

The turn doesn't help anyone and Schaefer is still the favorite.

Olson checks.
Schaefer also checks.

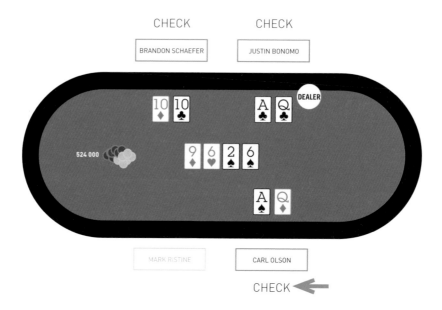

RIVER
K♦

The river doesn't change anything. But Schaefer now has a problem, because the river is an overcard to his ten. Schaefer can therefore lose if one of his opponents has a king.

Olson checks.
Schaefer also checks.
Bonomo shows first; his two opponents show their cards at the same time. Justin is eliminated, taking fourth place and winning $42,000.
Brandon Schaefer wins this hand.

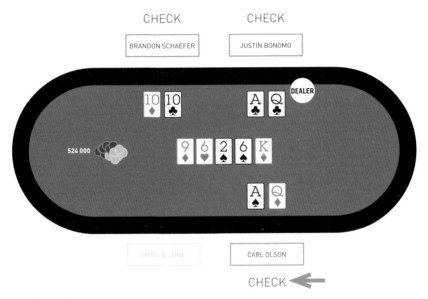

CONCLUSION

This hand shows it's possible, even recommended, to team up spontaneously against an opponent who has a smaller stack. (This kind of teamwork is called called implicit collusion.) Beginners might feel this is cheating, but, in No Limit Hold 'em, it's the size of the stack that sets the law: if, at any given time, a player has a smaller stack than his two opponents, he should be prepared for them to team up against him.

NOTE: No official deal can be made between two players. All agreements are to be tacit, as it is in this case. An official deal between two players immediately disqualifies them from playing.

Appendixes

POKER GLOSSARY

Ace-High: A five-card hand with an ace.

All-In: Betting all your chips, either to raise or call.

Ante: In seven-card stud, this is a forced bet before the deal begins. In button games (Texas Hold 'em, etc.) and at a certain tournament level, players pay an ante on top of the blind.

Backdoor: Completing a hand with the two last cards dealt (the turn and the river).

Bad Beat: Losing a game even though you were the favorite.

Bet the Pot: In pot limit games, this is the maximum bet. It is the amount in the pot.

Big Blind: 1) Forced bet provided before the deal by the player seated two seats after the button. 2) Player seated two seats after the button.

Blind Structure: For example $0.25/$0.50 means the small blind will be twenty-five cents and the big blind, fifty cents.

Blind: 1) Player to the left of the button. 2) A forced bet before the deal begins, provided by the player seated to the left of the button. There is also a small blind, or SB.

Bluff: Generic term for various strategies meant to lure in your opponent. A bluff is mainly accomplished through bets that contradict your hand. Bluffing is not only making your opponent believe you have a better hand than you do, sometimes it's doing the opposite (see slow-play).

Board: The community cards dealt on the flop, the turn and the river.

Bring-In: In the first round of seven-card stud, this is the forced bet paid by the lowest upcard.

Burn: Before the flop, the turn, or the river, the dealer discards one card (closed). This compensates for any deal errors.

Button: Chip (no value) designating the dealer's position.

Buy-In: Minimum amount required to sit down at a table or to play in a tournament.

Call: A bet that is the same amount as the preceding bet.

Cash Game: A hand directly involving money. In ordinary poker, as opposed to tournament poker, chips are used to represent money (each chip is designated a monetary value).

Check: To not bet. This is only possible if the betting has not started.

Check-Raise: A situation is which you call check, hope that someone else will open, and then raise in the same round.

Chip Leader: The player with the most chips at a table during a tournament.

Chip: The buy-in unit. Its value is determined at the beginning of the game.

Coin Flip: A situation in which you have about a one-in-two chance of winning.

Community Cards: Cards placed at the center of the table and shared by all players.

Connectors: Two consecutive cards, for example: 8–9

Deal In: Sitting at a table.

Deal Out: Leaving the table momentarily. In a tournament, the player who leaves the table still has to pay the blinds. This is not the case in cash games.

Down Cards, Pocket Cards: Hidden cards dealt to the player.

Draw: A potentially strong hand.

Drawing Dead: Drawing a card to complete a hand but to no avail.

Entry Fee: Commission on the tournament buy-in, for example: with $100 + $5, the entry fee is $5.

Family Pot: When the majority of players at a table are playing the hand, the pot is called a family pot.

Flop: The first three cards dealt to the board.

Flush Draw: Having four cards of the same suit and hoping to draw a fifth.

Fold: To quit the hand and lose your bets.

Free Roll: Tournament with no entry fee.

Hand: An action taking place between the ante or blind and the winning of the pot.

Heads Up: A poker game between two players or a head-to-head at the end of a tournament.

High Card: When there are no combinations in a hand, its value is equal to the highest rank card.

Hold 'Em: The same as Texas Hold 'em.

Hole cards: The cards dealt to a player, both hidden and visible.

Hunt: Forcing other players to fold through persistent raising.

Kicker: When one of the cards in your hand matches a card on the board, the second card in your hand is called a kicker.

Limit: Betting caps, determined from the start of the hand.

Limp In: Slow-playing before the flop and calling rather than raising after long consideration.

Muck: (1) The area where all the dead cards are placed. (2) To discard a hand.

No-Limit: Any game in which there is no limit on the size of the bet or the raise.

Nuts: When you have the best possible hand at the moment, you've got the nuts.

Odds: Probability of improving your hand. A one-in-four odds means you have a one-in-five chance of getting the card you want, that is, a 20 percent chance.

Omaha: In this poker variant, each player makes the best five-card hand with two of his four down cards and three of the five community cards.

Omaha High-Low: Omaha poker variation in which players aim to have the highest or lowest hand. The pot is split between the two.

Out: A card that will improve your hand.

Overcard: A card higher than any card on the board.

Overpair: A pocket pair that is higher than any card on the board.

Paint Card: A face card, that is, a Jack, Queen, or King.

Pocket Pair: Having a pair face down.

Poker Face: An expressionless and unemotional demeanor.

Pot Odds: Ratio of bet to pot. In other words, the win-to-loss ratio or risk-to-reward ratio.

Pot-Limit: Any game in which the maximum bet or raise is the size of the pot.

Prize Pool: Total funds in a tournament.

Rainbow: Three cards of three different suits.

Rake: Chips taken from the pot by a website or casino for hosting.

Read: Trying to figure out your opponent's hand.

Rebuy: In a rebuy tournament, buying a new buy-in. In cash games, buying more chips.

Re-raise: To raise an opponent's raise.

River: Fifth and last card on the board.

Rush: Winning several hands in a row. A winning streak.

Satellite: Tournament that qualifies you for a more expensive tournament.

Seven-Card Stud: In this poker variant, each player ends up with seven cards (three down, four up). The best five-card hand wins.

Seven-Card High Low: Seven-card stud variant in which players want the highest or lowest hand. The pot is split between the two.

Short Stack: The player with the smallest quantity of chips.

Showdown: When the remaining players after the last betting round expose their hands.

Sit and Go: A tournament that begins as soon as there are enough players.

Sit Out: To momentarily leave the table.

Slow Play: To not raise. To make an opponent believe you have a different hand.

Small Blind: See "Blind."

Split: The pot is split when there is a tie.

Spread Limit: The betting structure. For example, with 2–10, bets range between two and ten dollars.

Stack: The total number of chips a player has for betting.

Stand Up: To leave the table.

Steal the Pot: To win the pot when you don't have the best hand.

Straight Draw: Having four cards of consecutive rank and hoping to draw a fifth.

Suited Cards: Cards of the same suit.

Suited Connectors: Two consecutive cards of the same suit. For example: 8h–9h.

Table Stakes: Different forms of betting limits by which a player cannot bet more than what he/she has at the time of betting.

Tells: Signs that betray a player: tics, funny faces, looks, sweat, breathing, and so on.

Texas Hold 'Em: In this poker variant, the player is dealt two down cards. Then the five-card board is displayed. The player makes the best possible hand using his cards and the board.

Tight: A game without much action or a player who doesn't play many hands. As opposed to loose.

To Be on Tilt: Letting your emotions get the best of you.

Top Pair: The highest pair in the hand.

Tourney: Tournament.

Under the Gun (UTG): Being in the earliest position.

Up Cards: Community or personal cards that are visible to all players.

CHAT ROOM GLOSSARY

THIS CHAT ROOM GLOSSARY WILL FAMILIARIZE YOU WITH POKER'S SOCIAL SIDE. IT WILL HELP YOU TALK TO OTHER PLAYERS DURING THE HAND.
NOTE: SAVE FOR A FEW EXCEPTIONS, ABBREVIATIONS ARE WRITTEN IN LOWERCASE. WRITING IN ALL CAPS MEANS YOU'RE YELLING!

BB: big blind
ffs: for f*** sake!
gg: good game
gh: good hand
gl: good luck
gp: good play
gtg: got to go
he he: sniggering or giggling
IMO: In my opinion
lmao: laughing my ass off
lol: laugh out loud
nb: nice bet
nh: nice hand
omg: oh my God
pp: pocket pair
SB: small blind
sry: sorry (after a lucky break)
str8: straight
ul: unlucky
UTG: under the gun
uw: you wish
ty: thank you
tyvm: thank you very much
vnh: very nice hand
wp: well played
yw: you're welcome

POKER CHRONOLOGY

1820: A four-player betting game, played with twenty cards and no draws, becomes popular. Each player receives five cards and there are no bet limits.

1834: The word "poker" emerges. It most likely comes from the French *poque*, which is pronounced almost the same in English.

1837: The deck eventually consists of fifty-two cards.

1840–1845: The flush is introduced.

1845: The first rules of poker are published in *Hoyle's Games* by Henry F. Anners.

1850: Draw poker and wild cards are introduced. Raises are limited to three per round. The ante and blind are incorporated.

1855: The straight is gradually introduced. This hand is fully integrated starting in 1880.

1860: Table stakes are developed. Consequently, so are side pots (players cannot bet more than what they have on the table).

1863: The joker card is introduced.

1861–1865 (Civil War): Betting games are widespread, including five-card stud (which would really only become popular between 1920 and 1955) and seven-card stud. The historical version of poker, played with twenty cards and no draw, disappears.

1864: The first playing card symbols appear (the rank also appears at the corners).

1870: Card symbols face two ways, not just one way.

1870: Card corners are made round.

1872: Robert Cummings *Schenck's Poker Rules* is published. It is recognized as the first book to present the game's official rules. Jackpot poker, with a minimum bet, is introduced in Toledo, Ohio. The variant remains popular until 1950. The version that survives today is kill poker.

1891: First slot machine to use poker hands is developed.

1900–1905: Texas Hold'em is invented in Robstown, Texas.

1939–1945: Limit poker emerges.

1968: Texas Hold 'em is mentioned in the press for the first time.

1970: First official WSOP tournament.

1975: Video poker emerges.

1998: First online poker site is launched (PlanetPoker, then ParadisePoker).

1999: A poker tournament is televised for the first time (*Late Night Poker*).

WSOP CHAMPIONSHIP WINNERS

YEAR	NAME	WINNINGS	STARTING HAND	# OF PLAYERS
2006	JAMIE GOLD	$12,000,000	DP 9T	8773
2005	JOSEPH HACHEM	$7,500,000	7T 3P	5619
2004	GREG RAYMER	$5,000,000	8P 8K	2575
2003	CHRIS MONEYMAKER	$2,500,000	5K 4P	839
2002	ROBERT VARKONYI	$2,000,000	DK 10P	630
2001	CARLOS MORTENSEN	$1,500,000	RT DT	612
2000	CHRIS FERGUSON	$1,500,000	AP 9T	512
1999	NOEL FURLONG	$1,000,000	5T 5K	393
1998	SCOTTY NGUYEN	$1,000,000	VK 9T	350
1997	STU UNGAR	$1,000,000	AC 4T	312
1996	HUCK SEED	$1,000,000	9K 8K	295
1995	DAN HARRINGTON	$1,000,000	9K 8K	273
1994	RUSS HAMILTON	$1,000,000	RP 8C	240
1993	JIM BECHTEL	$1,000,000	VT 6C	220
1992	HAMID DASTMALCHI	$1,000,000	8C 4T	201
1991	BRAD DAUGHERTY	$1,000,000	RP VP	215
1990	MANSOUR MATLOUBI	$835,000	10K 10T	194
1989	PHIL HELLMUTH, JR.	$755,000	9P 9T	178
1988	JOHNNY CHAN	$700,000	VT 9T	167
1987	JOHNNY CHAN	$625,000	AP 9T	152
1986	BERRY JOHNSTON	$570,000	-	141
1985	BILL SMITH	$700,000	3P 3C	140
1984	JACK KELLER	$660,000	-	112
1983	TOM MCEVOY	$540,000	DK DP	108
1982	JACK STRAUS	$520,000	-	104
1981	STU UNGAR	$375,000	AC DC	75
1980	STU UNGAR	$365,000	5P 4P	73
1979	HAL FOWLER	$270,000	AC AT	54
1978	BOBBY BALDWIN	$210,000	-	42
1977	DOYLE BRUNSON	$340,000	10P 2C	34
1976	DOYLE BRUNSON	$220,000	10P 2P	22
1975	SAILOR ROBERTS	$210,000	9P 9C	22
1974	JOHNNY MOSS	$160,000	-	16
1973	PUGGY PEARSON	$130,000	AP 7P	13
1972	AMARILLO PRESTON	$80,000	-	8
1971	JOHNNY MOSS	$30,000	-	6
1970	JOHNNY MOSS	PLAYERS VOTES	-	7

WPT CUMULATED WINNINGS

RANK	WINNINGS	# VICTORIES
01. TUAN LE	$4,467,738	2
02. DANIEL NEGREANU	$4,259,340	2
03. MICHAEL MIZRACHI	$3,988,230	2
04. ALAN GOEHRING	$3,785,528	2
05. JOSEPH BARTHOLDI	$3,760,165	1
06. MARTIN DE KNIJFF	$2,810,168	1
07. HASAN HABIB	$2,409,504	0
08. ERICK LINDGREN	$2,243,351	2
09. NICHOLAS SCHULMAN	$2,192,500	2
10. GUS HANSEN	$2,171,546	3
11. REHNE PEDERSEN	$2,166,060	1
12. DOYLE BRUNSON	$1,980,347	1
13. DAVID MATTHEW	$1,903,950	0
14. BARRY GREENSTEIN	$1,863,594	2
15. GAVIN SMITH	$1,742,233	1
16. SCOTTY NGUYEN	$1,713,409	1
17. PAUL MAXFIELD	$1,711,460	0
18. ROLAND DE WOLFE	$1,648,955	1
19. MICHAEL GRACZ	$1,645,906	1
20. HUMBERTO BRENES	$1,613,445	0
21. VICTOR RAMDIN	$1,604,387	1
22. JOHN STOLZMANN	$1,511,282	1
23. AL ARDEBILI	$1,504,650	1
24. ANTONIO ESFANDIARI	$1,500,135	1
25. PAUL PHILLIPS	$1,499,005	1
26. STEVE PAUL-AMBROSE	$1,407,035	1
27. HOYT CORKINS	$1,398,990	1
28. NAM LE	$1,340,767	1
29. FREDDY DEEB	$1,310,828	1
30. PATRIK ANTONIUS	$1,238,235	0
31. LEE WATKINSON	$1,166,807	0
32. DANIEL QUACH	$1,162,560	0
33. PHIL IVEY	$1,153,796	0
34. JUAN CARLOS MORTENSEN	$1,148,645	1
35. ALEX KAHANER	$1,125,900	0
36. SURINDER SUNAR	$1,111,570	1
37. JOHN D'AGOSTINO	$1,111,384	0
38. BILL GAZES	$1,094,913	0
39. TED FORREST	$1,091,215	0
40. MINH LY	$1,060,050	1
41. MIKE SIMON	$1,052,890	1
42. ALL IN TONY LICASTRO	$1,035,000	0
43. DANNY NGUYEN	$1,025,000	1
44. ELI ELEZRA	$1,024,574	1
45. ERIC BRENES	$1,000,000	1
46. DAVID MINTO	$1,000,000	0

TEXAS HOLD 'EM ODDS

In poker, you have to be able to accurately evaluate your chances of winning so that you can decide whether to fold or to raise. Luckily, there are recurring situations in Texas Hold 'em, so knowing your odds is much easier.

Many players don't have a hold on these numbers, which gives a great advantage to opponents who do. Knowing your odds means you can fold when your chances of winning are slim, and stay in when your chances are decent. An inexperienced player, who does not calculate probabilities, will make many more mistakes.

In Limit, odds are key. In No Limit Hold 'em, they're a bit less important because a player can compensate by being aggressive or mentally sharp. For example, he might be particularly precise at "reading" his opponent.

ASSESSING YOUR HAND

This table lays out your chances of having a certain hand before the flop.

ODDS OF HAVING	PERCENTAGE
Suited cards	24 %
Ace	14 %
Connectors	16 %
Two face cards	9 %
Pair	6 %
Suited connectors	4 %
Top three hands (AA-KK-AK)	2 %
Ace-king	1 %
Two aces	0.5 %

When You Have Two Cards of Different Ranks, the Probability of Flopping

Pair	27 %
A pair or better	32 %

When You Have a Pair, the Probability of Flopping

Three of a kind	12 %
A three-of-a-kind or better	13 %

When You Have Suited Connectors, the Probability of Flopping

Straight or flush	2 %
Straight draw or flush draw	20 %
Pair	27 %

When You Start with a Pair, the Probability of Making by the End of the Hand

Three of a kind	12 %
Flush	2 %
Full house	9 %

REMEMBER:

- The chances of being dealt a pair of aces is one in two hundred twenty. (If you're playing live, you'll be dealt a pair of aces on average every seven hours).
- The chances of being dealt two cards higher than ten is one in eleven.
- The chances of being dealt at least one ace is one in seven.

ACE PREFLOP

This table lays out your chances of being the only player to have an ace. Your odds depend on the number of players in the hand.

# OF PLAYERS	PROBABILITY OF BEING THE ONLY PLAYER WITH AN ACE	PROBABILITY THAT NO PLAYER HAS ONE
2	88 %	85 %
3	77 %	70 %
4	68 %	59 %
5	59 %	50 %
6	50 %	40 %
7	43 %	32 %
8	36 %	26 %
9	31 %	20 %
10	25 %	16 %

REMEMBER

- In heads-up, you don't have to worry that your opponent has an ace. Eight out of ten times, neither of you will have one.
- Against at least six players, the chances that someone else also has an ace is better than one in two.
- With a full table, if five players see the flop, a player is likely to have an ace better than one in two times.

ASSESSING THE FLOP

This table lays out the odds against flopping the following community cards.

FLOP	PERCENTAGE
Two different suits	55 %
Three different suits	40 %
Connectors	40 %
Pair	16 %
Three suited cards	5 %
Three consecutive cards	3,5 %
Ace-King	1 %
Two Kings	0.5 %
Three-of-a-kind	0.3 %

REMEMBER

- There is a pair on the flop one in five times.
- There is a pair before the river one in two times.
- There are two suited cards on the flop more than one in two times.
- When three players are contesting the hand, and the board has two cards of the same suit, 60 percent of the time one player will hold two cards of this same suit.
- There are three suited cards on the flop one in twenty times.
- There are three cards of the same rank on the flop one in four hundred twenty-five times.

THE HAND PLAYABILITY THEORY

This table recaps hand playability with regard to your position.

- All Positions
- End Position
- Middle/End Position
- Unplayable

Pairs and suited cards

A-A	A-J	K-Q	Q-J	J-T	T-9	9-8	9-7	7-6	6-5	5-4	4-3	3-2
K-K	A-Q	K-J	Q-T	J-9	T-8	9-7	8-6	7-5	6-4	5-3	4-2	
Q-Q	A-J	K-T	Q-9	J-8	T-7	9-6	8-5	7-4	6-3	5-2		
J-J	A-T	K-9	Q-8	J-7	T-6	9-5	8-4	7-3	6-2			
T-T	A-9	K-8	Q-7	J-6	T-5	9-4	8-3	7-2				
9-9	A-8	K-7	Q-6	J-5	T-4	9-3	8-2					
8-8	A-7	K-6	Q-5	J-4	T-3	9-2						
7-7	A-6	K-5	Q-4	J-3	T-2							
6-6	A-5	K-4	Q-3	J-2								
5-5	A-4	K-3	Q-2									
4-4	A-3	K-2										
3-3	A-2											
2-2												

Offsuit cards

A-K	K-Q	Q-J	J-T	T-9	9-8	8-7	7-6	6-5	5-4	4-3	3-2
A-Q	K-J	Q-T	J-9	T-8	9-7	8-6	7-5	6-4	5-3	4-2	
A-J	K-T	Q-9	J-8	T-7	9-6	8-5	7-4	6-3	5-2		
A-T	K-9	Q-8	J-7	T-6	9-5	8-4	7-3	6-2			
A-9	K-8	Q-7	J-6	T-5	9-4	8-3	7-2				
A-8	K-7	Q-6	J-5	T-4	9-3	8-2					
A-7	K-6	Q-5	J-4	T-3	9-2						
A-6	K-5	Q-4	J-3	T-2							
A-5	K-4	Q-3	J-2								
A-4	K-3	Q-2									
A-3	K-2										
A-2											

CALCULATING OUTS AFTER THE FLOP

Outs represent the number of cards that will improve your hand. For example, there are eight outs to improve your straight draw to a straight. This number is key in estimating the odds of improving your hand.

• After the flop: use the chart below to calculate the probability of improving your hand with either one or two cards to come. After the flop, multiply the number of outs by four to figure out the probability of improving your hand if you see both the turn and the river.

• After the turn or to figure out your odds card by card after the flop, multiply the number of outs by two to figure out the improvement ratio.

# OF IMPROVING CARDS (OUTS)	TWO CARDS TO COME	ONE CARD TO COME (TURN OR RIVER)
21(double draw + 2 overcards)	70 %	45 %
20	68	43
19	65	40
18 (double draw + 1 overcard)	62	38
17	60	36
16	57	34
15 (flush draw, straight draw)	54	32
14	51	30
13	48	28
12	45	26
11 (flush draw + pair)	42	24
10 (straight draw + pair)	38	22
9 (flush draw)	35	20
8 (straight draw)	32	17
7	28	15
6	24	13
5	20	11
4 (2 pair)	17	9
3	13	7
2	8	4
1	4	2

Note for Over Ten Outs

• When you calculate with only one card to come, the approximation is slightly *less* in reality.

• When you calculate with two cards to come, the approximation is *higher* than in reality; the real number is obtained by removing 1 percent per out. For example: 15 outs = 60 percent-5=55 percent (in fact, 54 percent).

PROBABILITY OF IMPROVING AFTER THE FLOP

This table lays out the odds against improving your hand after the flop.

YOU HAVE:	YOU COULD END UP WITH:	%
Four suited cards	Flush	35 %
Trips	Full house or four of a kind	33 %
Open straight draw	Straight	32 %
Two pair	Full house or four-of-a-kind	17 %
Pair	Three of a kind, full house	8 %

ODDS OF WINNING AT THE SHOWDOWN

This table lays out the odds of winning at the showdown when there are two or ten players.

HAND	TWO PLAYERS (HEADS UP)	TEN PLAYERS (FULL TABLE)
Two aces	85 %	31 %
Two kings	82 %	26 %
Two queens	80 %	22 %
Two jacks	77 %	19 %
Pair of tens	75 %	17 %
Pair of nines	72 %	15 %
Pair of eights	69 %	14 %
Suited ace-kin:	67 %	21 %
Pair of sevens	66 %	13 %
Suited ace-queen	66 %	19 %
Suited ace-jack	65 %	18 %

REMEMBER

- The value of a draw is greater the more players there are.
- The value of a pair is greater the fewer players there are, except for a pair of threes and twos, which have greater value the higher the number of players contesting the pot.
- With ten players, a pair of aces will only win 31 percent of the time, that is less than one in three; a pair of kings will only win one in four, etc. Make sure to protect this hand by raising preflop in order to narrow the field and increase your odds of winning the hand, preventing an opponent with an inferior hand from outdrawing you.

ASSESSING THE FINAL BOARD

This table presents the odds of the final board showing any of the combinations below.

THE BOARD	PERCENTAGE
Better than a pair	50 %
Pair	42 %
Four consecutive cards	17 %
Gut shot straight draw	9 %
Four suited cards	5 %

PREFLOP DUELS

This page lays out the odds of winning the pot when players go all-in before the flop.

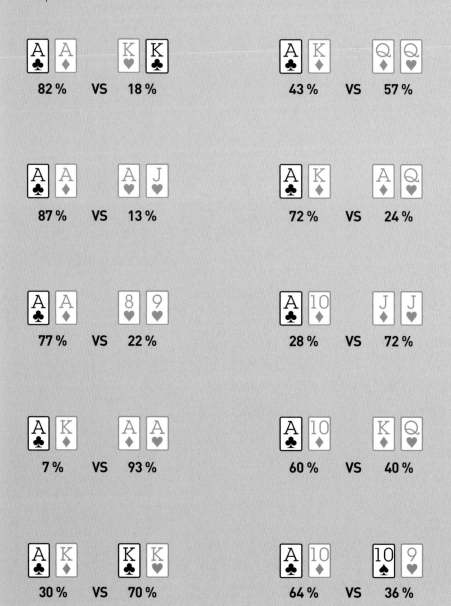

A♣ A♦ K♥ K♣
82 % **VS** 18 %

A♣ K♦ Q♦ Q♥
43 % **VS** 57 %

A♣ A♦ A♥ J♥
87 % **VS** 13 %

A♣ K♦ A♦ Q♥
72 % **VS** 24 %

A♣ A♦ 8♥ 9♥
77 % **VS** 22 %

A♣ 10♦ J♦ J♥
28 % **VS** 72 %

A♣ K♦ A♦ A♥
7 % **VS** 93 %

A♣ 10♦ K♦ Q♥
60 % **VS** 40 %

A♣ K♦ K♣ K♥
30 % **VS** 70 %

A♣ 10♦ 10♠ 9♥
64 % **VS** 36 %

DUELS ON THE FLOP

Once the flop is turned over, five of the seven cards a player can use to make the best possible hand have been exposed. The way your hand matches the flop will greatly influence your upcoming strategy.

Made Hands   ## Draws

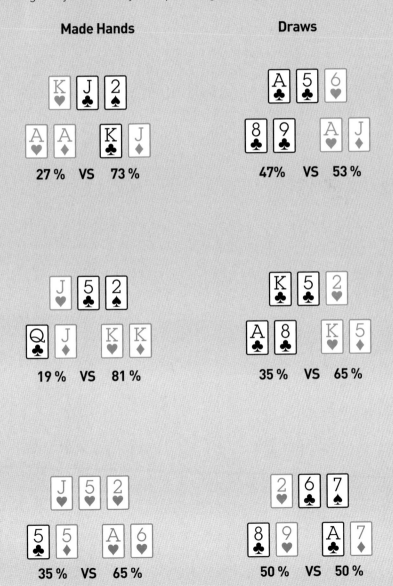

Made Hands

K♥ J♣ 2♠
A♥ A♦   K♣ J♦
27% VS 73%

J♥ 5♣ 2♠
Q♣ J♦   K♥ K♦
19% VS 81%

J♥ 5♥ 2♥
5♣ 5♦   A♥ 6♥
35% VS 65%

Draws

A♣ 5♣ 6♥
8♣ 9♣   A♥ J♦
47% VS 53%

K♣ 5♣ 2♥
A♣ 8♣   K♥ 5♦
35% VS 65%

2♥ 6♣ 7♠
8♣ 9♥   A♣ 7♦
50% VS 50%

POKER FILMOGRAPHY

Naïs
1945, directed by Raymond Leboursier, with Fernandel and Jacqueline Pagnol
The Mississippi Gambler
1953, directed by Rudolph Maté, with Tyrone Power
The Man with the Golden Arm
1955, directed by Otto Preminger, with Frank Sinatra and Kim Novak
The Rawhide Years
1956, directed by Rudolph Maté, with Tony Curtis
Cheyenne Autumn
1964, directed by John Ford, with James Stewart
The Cincinnati Kid
1965, directed by Norman Jewison, with Steve McQueen, Edward G. Robinson, and Ann-Margret
Frankie and Johnny
1966, directed by Frederick de Cordova, with Elvis Presley
Once Upon a Time in the West
1969, directed by Sergio Leone, with Henry Fonda and Charles Bronson
The Sting
1973, directed by George Roy Hill, with Robert Redford and Paul Newman
Regalo di natale (Christmas Present)
1986, directed by Pupi Avati
Poker
1987, directed by Catherine Corsini, with Pierre Arditi
House of Games
1987, directed by David Mamet, with Lindsay Crouse, Joe Mantegna, and Lilia Skala
Poker Alice
1987, directed by Arthur Allan Seidelman, with Elizabeth Taylor
Havana
1990, directed by Sydney Pollack, with Robert Redford and Lena Olin
Maverick
1994, directed by Richard Donner, with Mel Gibson, Jodie Foster, and James Coburn
Lock, Stock and Two Smoking Barrels
1998, directed by Guy Ritchie, with Dexter Fletcher, Jason Flemyng, and Steven Mackintosh
Rounders
1998, directed by John Dahl, with Matt Damon, Edward Norton, and John Turturro
Shade
2003, directed by Damian Nieman, with Sylvester Stallone and Thandie Newton
Casino Royale
2006, directed by Martin Campbell, with Daniel Craig and Eva Green
Lucky You
2007, directed by Curtis Hanson, with Eric Bana, Drew Barrymore and Robert Duvall

POKER BIBLIOGRAPHY

STRATEGY BOOKS

Super System:
How I Made Over $1,000,000
Playing Poker
Doyle Brunson (1980)

Super System 2
Doyle Brunson (2004)

Harrington on Hold'em
Dan Harrington & Bill Robertie
(2004)

Ace on the River
Barry Greenstein (2005)

Book of Tells:
Body Language of Poker
Mike Caro (Gambling Times 1984)

Play Poker, Quit Work
and Sleep Till Noon!
John Fox (1977)

Tournament Practice Hands
Tom McEvoy & T. J. Cloutier (2003)

Theory of Poker
David Sklansky (1987)

1000 Best Poker Strategies
and Secrets
Susie Isaacs (2006)

Les trucs au poker
Robert Bagnoli (De Vecchi 1982)

Championship Tournament Poker
Tom McEvoy (1996, 2005)

Poker Cadillac
François Montmirel
(Fantaisium 2006)

The Rules of Poker: Essentials for
Every Game
Lou Krieger (2005)

Poker On Line
François Montmirel (2006)

L'Illusion du Hasard
Alexis Beuve (1997)

OTHER BOOKS

Positively Fifth Street
James McManus (2003)

Gambling Collectibles
Leonard Schneir (1993)

Total Poker
David Spanier (1977, 1990)

La Brigade des jeux
André Burnat
(Presses de la cité 1977)

The Biggest Game in Town
A. Alvarez (1963)

Education of a Poker Player
Herbert O. Yardley (1957)

Big Deal
Anthony Holden (1990)

Oscar and Lucinda
Peter Carey (1990)

Poker d'âmes
Tim Powers (1992)

The Cincinnati Kid
Richard Jessup (1963)

Havana
Paul Monette (1991)

The Sting
Robert Weverka (1974)

The Music of Chance
Paul Auster (1991)

La gagne
Bernard Lentéric (1980)

Piqué de poker
Philippe Balland (1989)

Easy Money
Patrick Green (1996)

Parodie
Cizia Zykë (1987)

La Grande Arnaque
Leonard Wise (1977)

**Un oursin sur les tapis verts:
Impair et passe**
Philippe Bouvard (1975)

Poker pour l'enfer
Jacques Demar (1967)

Brelan de Nippons
Tito Topin (1982)

Rachel la Dame de carreau
Michel Steiner (2000)

Poker Sauvage
Mark Joseph (2001)

Le poker du capitaine Leslie
Bernard Gorsky (1975)

Poker d'enfer
S. A. Steeman (1955)

Le Flambeur
Noël Vexin (1958)

L'Aristo chez les tricheurs
André Helena (1954)

Blue Hotel
Stephen Crane (2003)

La dernière peut-être
Daniel Berkowicz (2000)

Voyage au pays du jeu
Louis-André (1934)

Comment on nous vole
Eugène Villiod (1906)

Strip Poker
André Burnat (1984)

POKER WEB SITES

Poker Portals and Blogs

www.pokerlistings.com
www.pokerpulse.com
www.whichpoker.com
www.cardplayer.com
www.pokerineurope.com
www.pokernews.com
www.pokerpages.com
www.thehendonmob.com

Learn to Play and Improve Your Game

www.diyforum.org/table
www.freerolls.drawdead.com
www.fulltiltpoker.com/prolessons.php
www.gocee.com/poker
www.holdemsecrets.com
www.homepokergames.com
www.homepokertourney.com/
www.internettexasholdem.com
www.live.checknraisepoker.com
www.playwinningpoker.com
www.poker-babes.com
www.pokerpages.com
www.pokersavvy.com
www.pokerstrategyforum.com
www.pokertips.org
www.pokerworks.com
www.recpoker.com
www.school-poker.com
www.susieisaacs.com/limitededitions.htm
www.texasholdem-poker.com
www.thegoodgamblingguide.co.uk/
www.games.com/poker.htm
www.unitedpokerforum.com

Experts and Players

Josh Arieh - www.josharieh.com
Andy Bloch - www.andybloch.com
Mike Caro - www.poker1.com
Bob Ciaffone - www.pokercoach.us
Annie Duke - www.annieduke.com
Chris Ferguson- www.chrisferguson.com
Gus Hansen - www.gus-hansen.com
Jennifer Harman-www.jenniferharman.com
Phil Hellmuth - www.philhellmuth.com
Phil Ivey - www.philivey.com
John Juanda - www.johnjuanda.com
Lou Krieger - www.loukrieger.com
Howard Lederer-www.howardlederer.com
Liz Lieu - www.lizlieu.net
Erick Lindgren - www.ericklindgren.com
Chris Moneymaker - www.chrismoney-maker.com
Daniel Negreanu-www.fullcontactpoker.com
Evelyn Ng - www.evybabee.com
Greg Raymer - www.fossilmanpoker.com
Shirley Rosario - www.poker-babes.com
Rolf Slotboom - www.rolfslotboom.com
David "Devilfish" Ulliott - www.devilfish-poker.com

INDEX

PHOTO CREDITS

▬ ◆ ◆ ◆ ▬

Authors
FRANÇOIS MONTMIREL
With the contribution from
Nicolas Marçais and Philippe Marchand

Editorial conception
Nicolas Marçais and Philippe Marchand

Graphic design
www.olo-olo.com

Page-setting
Mehdi Lajnef

Photo research
Eve Zheim

Rewriting
Odile Zimmermann

Acknowledgments
Sabine Arqué-Greenberg,
David Ausseil, Chris Collier,
Emilie Greenberg, Manuela Kerkoff,
Nicolas Marchand, Hervé Martin
Delpierre, Hedwige Pasquet,
Frédérique Sarfati, Marc Walter,
as well as the SLOP : Cédric, Céline,
Jérôme, Jean-François, Mercedes,
Oléastre, Olivier, PIB, Pierre, Xavier...

Printed in Singapore
By Tien Wah Press

Created by
www.ultimate-book.com